On The Potter's Wheel

PRINCIPLES TO LIVE BY IN A CRISIS DRIVEN WORLD
LESSONS I LEARNED THROUGH ADVERSITY

Teresita Glasgow

IN HIS SEASON, INC. PUBLISHING
POWDER SPRING, GEORGIA

Copyright © 2019 by Teresita Glasgow.

All rights reserved. No part of this publication may be reproduced, distributed or transmitted in any form or by any means, including photocopying, recording, or other electronic or mechanical methods, without the prior written permission of the publisher, except in the case of brief quotations embodied in critical reviews and certain other noncommercial uses permitted by copyright law. For permission requests, write to the publisher, addressed "Attention: Permissions Coordinator," at the address below.

Teresita Glasgow/In His Season, Inc. Publishing
www.inhisseason,com
www.teresitaglasgow.com
www.destinydreamercoaching.com

Ordering Information:
Special discounts are available on quantity purchases by churches, corporations, associations, and others. For details, contact the "Special Sales Department" at (404) 973-0281or info@inhisseason.com.

On The Potter's Wheel/ Teresita Glasgow
ISBN-13: 978-0-578-45446-7
ISBN-10: 0-57845446-7

Contents

Dedication i

Prologue v

Part I

Chapter One: In The Beginning God 1

Chapter Two: Reflections-Looking back can be good 27

Chapter Three: Introspection-Taking a look inside 59

Part II

Chapter Four: The Process Can be Painful 75

Chapter Five: Coming to Terms 91

Chapter Six: Embracing The Change 103

Part III

Chapter Seven: Understanding What You've Learned .. 125

Chapter Eight: New Beginnings 151

The Conclusion 159

About the Author 160

ON THE POTTER'S WHEEL • II

Dedication

This book is dedicated to an Omnipotent, Omnipresent, and Omniscient God who loves us too much to allow us to fail.

"The word which came to Jeremiah from the Lord, saying, arise, and go down to the potter's house, and there I will cause *thee to hear my words. Then I went down to the potter's house, and, behold, he wrought a work on the wheels. And the vessel that he made of clay was marred in the hand of the potter: so he made it again another vessel, as seemed good to the potter to make it."*

—JEREMIAH 18:1-4 (King James Version)

Prologue

This book is about suffering loss and the road to recovery; introspection, reflection and recovery. Suffering loss is not rare; most people within their lifetime will come face to face with loss. Death, divorce, illness, or a job loss can all have a negative impact. Within these pages I share, very transparently my loss. Some may say that my loss was not serious but I can assure you that for me it was as serious as death (although, it probably should not have been). But, it is the internal work that I did on myself, the spiritual and practical principles that I learned along the way that I hope will help you.

Some years ago an event took place in my life that had the potential to devastate me and to destroy my family. For me, it was nothing short of catastrophic. I did not realize it at the time but this event would have an impact on my life that would usher in a drastic directional change to my future. This event meant that my life would be different and that I would be forever changed. It made a difference in what I believed and why I believed it. It initiated my willingness to participate in a process that was a part of the directional change that I had to take to reach my destiny. It changed how I gathered information and how I processed and used that information that I gathered. It changed what was important to me and what didn't matter anymore. In the final analysis, it pointed me in the direction that God had ordained for me before the foundation of the world.

Some people say that "time heals all wounds" but in reality, time does not heal at all, time is only an ingredient that God uses. Sometimes the agent of time is used by God while He carries out His work. When it comes to emotional issues, financial situations and sometimes physical healing, time can be a vital element used by God. I once heard a statement that said "You didn't get into this overnight and it's for sure you won't get out of it overnight," that saying has taken on new meaning to me because the journey that I embarked on lasted over a period of years and even now, I realize that where I am is a continuation of where I've been and where I've yet to go. This book chronicles some of the challenges, opportunities and vital lessons that I learned during that period.

In the beginning I thought that this situation would go away quickly, but it didn't. I thought that it would not be painful, but it was. I thought that I knew God, but I found that I didn't know Him as well as I thought that I did. Although, at the time of this event, I'd had a personal relationship with God for over twenty years, I guess that I could describe my attitude like that of a teenager with a parent, cocky and too familiar. I would not have considered myself a "spiritual baby" but what I found out was that I also was not exactly spiritually mature either. Much of my spiritual knowledge had never been tested or proven; I'd never encountered a situation that called for me to exercise the things that I had been taught, it was more head knowledge than heart knowledge and the level of faith that I was operating in at the time was not sufficient for the next phase of my journey in life.

There comes a point in every child's life when a parent allows the child more freedom to see if they will use the lessons that they have been taught. But, no loving parent will allow a child to go too far without correction and instruction. God used this time to develop my character and to show me areas of spiritual and emotional immaturity in my life; He also helped me to understand why those areas in my life existed. Although I was born again for a long time and had made substantial growth in terms of my spirituality I mean, I understood who I was in Christ Jesus, I tithed and regularly attended and volunteered at church, but, to my surprise, when I thought that God would back me up on some of the decisions that I made toward my career, He didn't. I was surprised by His seeming abandonment but my love for Him helped me to submit to Him when things went contrary to my expectations.

I'd had many challenges in my life and God had always gotten me through them. He never let me down before and I knew that He wouldn't let me down now but I was concerned because I didn't understand why He allowed this to happen.

I realize now that God saw areas in my life that I was unaware of that needed to be changed. Some of these areas were buried so deeply and for so long that I had no idea that they existed. Things from my past that I thought were gone weren't gone at all but, were buried deep beneath the surface and the enemy knew it and used it.

Before this event happened, I was comfortable and successful, if anyone had asked me at the time if I were in my purpose, I would have said yes. I didn't realize that everything that had taken place in my life up to that point was merely training for God's real purpose for my life.

I was about to realize my God given purpose but before I could realize it, I had to undergo a process of change. That change could only come when I learned to think differently. Although the change would be painful, I knew that without it, I would not be able to move forward in my life. I learned that I had hidden areas that needed to be uprooted. Although it was not like starting over, it was more like going to another level, but it seemed like I was starting all over again.

In reality, what the enemy told me was failure wasn't failure at all, it was a severe shift in direction.

If I understood at the time that the shift was going to be used by God, maybe I would not have resisted the change, but for reasons that I will discuss later, for these reasons, I was placed on the potter's wheel.

Part I

CHAPTER 1

In the Beginning God

THE ENCOUNTER

In the beginning God, these are the words that stood out in my mind after I was summoned by my manager to a conference room in the bank where I worked. For about two years the environment in the office had become increasingly hostile, and I didn't care anymore what the outcome of this meeting would be, I was tired. I knew that I had done everything possible to comply with my manager's request; I knew that nothing that I did would satisfy her, she wanted me out. I was determined to trust God knowing that He would help me to get through this no matter what they decided to do.

The weekend prior to this meeting, I had attended an Encounter with the church that I attended. The Encounter was a two day meeting held in a remote location, it was a time away from life's daily routines; a time to pray, reflect, meditate and to be taught the Word of God. There were no televisions, radios or any other distractions that would stop me from reaching my goal. The goal of the Encounter was to encounter God, the other attendees and myself. When the weekend was over, I had reached the goal because I had encountered God the other attendees and more importantly, I had encountered myself and I was not happy with everything that I saw.

I knew after the Encounter that I needed to return to my office and to apologize to my manager. The apology was not as much for her as it was for me, I didn't think that she would care about the apology or that she would accept it. But, I knew that it was the right thing for me to do. During the Encounter, I was able to see my own rebellion and pride. For the first time in months, it was clear to me, that regardless of my manager's actions, I was obligated by my faith in Jesus Christ to respect her authority and I wasn't sure that I had always done that according to the Word. It wasn't until I heard a man of God explain the difference between authority and control that I fully understood that it was not the authority that I rebelled against but it was my manager's desire to exert control over me. The Holy Spirit is the only one we are to give complete control! I was willing to submit to her authority but I was not willing to submit to her control.

While authority and control are different, I did not know that at the time, therefore I was responsible for what I did know. I was never disrespectful and I was always productive and contributed to the bottom line whenever I was allowed to. The problem was that my manager didn't like competition and in her mind, I guess, I had become competition, although that was the farthest thing from my mind. My manager became a "micro manager" and she became someone that it was impossible to have a productive conversation with.

> *"Servants, be obedient to them that are your masters according to the flesh, with fear and trembling, in singleness of your heart, as unto Christ; Not with eye service, as menpleasers; but as the servants of Christ, doing the will of God from the heart; With good will doing service, as to the Lord, and not to men: Knowing that whatsoever good thing any man doeth, the same shall he receive of the Lord, whether he be bond or free"~ Ephesians 6:5-8*

I never had a manager like this one before, her insecurity and need for power combined with her management style ran right into my own strongly independent and autonomous working style. In the past, my work style had always been received positively; a real plus and it had led to promotions. I had a reputation as a "can do, team player. Now, the very things that had always been considered by my other employers as an asset had become a liability. I tried on every occasion at first to work with my manager and to work based on her style, I realized after a while that even that was not working. Eventually, I became offended when I realized that she was trying to push me out. I had no desire to leave the position and I thought that she would get over it.

Thinking about it now, I know that my stubborn decision to stay in the position was rooted in fear and not in faith. Although at the time, I believed that I was in faith and that I was resisting the devil and taking my stand but just the opposite was true. I knew that I wanted to stay in Georgia and that the choice of jobs in my industry was slim to non-existent. I became another of my manager's targets for extinction. This was her modus operandi; there was a long line of people, my predecessors, who also had undergone this treatment. I reasoned that my situation was different because God was on my side.

All testing is based on resistance and I was about to be tested and tried. In James 4:7 the scripture says to "resist the devil and he will flee from you", No it doesn't, it actually says" submit yourselves therefore to God; resist the devil and he will flee from you." This means that to the degree or the direct proportion that you are willing to submit to God, is the degree to which you will be able to resist the devil. I realized during the Encounter that I was exhausted and I couldn't tell submitting to God from resisting the devil or walking in faith from walking in fear, I was tired. I learned that it is difficult to walk in faith when you are tired. My ability to reason suffered from the treatment that I had endured. I learned that sometimes it's good to disconnect and get away from everything. I know now that this is why Jesus withdrew from the crowd to replenish, which is what the Encounter did for me. I didn't realize how exhausted I was until the Encounter.

Before the Encounter my prayers were based more on my emotions and the mistreatment than on the Word of God. I didn't realize that my faith was not working until I was confronted on the Encounter with my own mistakes. Faith works by love and because I was so deeply offended, my faith couldn't work. My attempts to walk in love didn't work because I was just pretending; my heart was not in it. I started out right but over a period of time, I began to resent my manager. I went to work every day knowing that the day would be an obstacle course that she would use every weapon in her arsenal to make my life miserable.

One of my favorite passages in the bible is the Sermon on the Mount the "Be Attitudes" or the "Attitudes to Be" in Matthew 5:1-16 but, when I was faced with the tactics that my manager used, I found out that turning the other cheek was not an easy thing to do. I had arrived at a place and time where it was difficult for me to be everything that God expected me to be. I wasn't even operating at a level of my own expectations, I was tired. God seemed a little different to me now too because although I prayed and prayed, things did not go the way that I thought that they should have gone in this situation

But now, after the Encounter, I knew that I needed to make some adjustments.

During the Encounter I realized that God did not fit into the neat little box that I had put Him in, and that I had not understood His ways during this particular circumstance. I expected God to move in this circumstance in a way that was contrary to His Word. It never occurred to me that my murmuring and complaining had shut Him out of the situation, He hates murmuring and complaining, even when you think you're right! All that I could see was the emotional pressure cooker that I was in, I couldn't see that my own actions were working against the situation; I failed to take the "time out" that I needed to put everything into perspective. I allowed pride to tell me that I could fight the situation when the battle wasn't mine, it was the Lord's. So I prayed to God but my heart was full of offence. I went to work every day and worked as hard as I could to prove that I could handle the pressure but the pressure only escalated.

I think that because of God's love for me; He used this experience to reveal Himself to me in a way that I had not known Him before. I think that my faith grew during this time in a way that it can only grow during times of opposition, discomfort and difficulty. I went to a new level of spiritual maturity after the Encounter, a new dimension of trust and faith. I had to conquer the things that were inside of me, the ideas and beliefs that could not go with me to the next level. It never occurred to me that I needed to go through this battle or that God could use this situation to develop a deeper level of intimacy with Him. It never occurred to me that God was directing my path. This experience was unlike any other that I had gone through in the past. It was a new day, a new assignment, but I continued to cling to the old and the familiar. My focus was on staying with and keeping my old blessing and God wanted to bless me with something new. My thinking needed to change but I was clueless up until the Encounter and God seemed to be silent.

How Did I Get Here?

When the bank that I worked for on Wall Street, in New York acquired a book of Corporate Trust business accounts in Atlanta, Georgia, I was relocated there by the bank. My assignment was to help the new employees learn the bank's policies, procedures and computer systems while performing my duties as a Corporate Trust relationship manager. My other duties included establishing new relationships and closing bond deals.

Senior management arranged for me to relocate and I knew that another promotion was in my future.

Upon my arrival to the Atlanta office, I found that my coming from the New York office was not something that the Atlanta staff wanted although, I had flown down and interviewed with them prior to making the decision to relocate. During the meeting everyone seemed pleased at my coming but when I arrived, that changed they saw me as an outsider and treated me as such. No matter how hard I tried the relationships remained strained. The day to day work was fine and there were some good occasions but it was clear that they had made up their minds that I should remain an outsider. By this time in my career I had been involved in several mergers and acquisitions of Corporate Trust businesses and I knew it could be difficult for the prior staff. I attributed their attitudes to the feelings employees have when a company they have been loyal to sells the business to someone else with little or no regard for their wellbeing I didn't take it personally.

A year later when I was made an offer of employment by another bank in Atlanta, I accepted the offer and quickly left my former employer. I had worked with for them for six years in New York and Atlanta. I thought that the situation at the new position would be more welcoming and it also came with a promotion and an increase in pay. But, as my grandmother would say "I went from the frying pan into the skillet." At first, things were great for me but I noticed that another woman there was having a problem with my new manager.

It soon became apparent to me that I had been hired as this woman's replacement although she had not vacated her position yet! Not a good sign. At first my manager was very supportive of everything that I did but things began to sour when I rejected some of the things that she did. I did not always agree with her and I believed that my opinion mattered. I was not used to working in a "My way or the highway" environment. In the banks where I had worked everyone could voice their opinions and allow management to make to final decision. I was hired based on my experience and reputation so I didn't believe that I was supposed to dummy down.

I was used to sharing my opinions and expressing myself when I thought a situation needed to be addressed. Good communication skills are part of a senior corporate position but this manager was only interested in one opinion, hers. The nature of Corporate Trust required that I work independently and interdependently within a team environment. Meaning I handled my accounts but also helped others as needed and participated in team meetings and activities.

On the surface, the office was organized the same way, each of us had a book of business but we also interacted with one another as a team. The problem in this office was it was a façade. The management style caused the place to operate under a cloud. Each time a person was hired at the level that I held, it was only a matter of time before my manager became paranoid and began to abuse her position. The people in the position before me all eventually left the bank. But unlike my predecessors, I decided to stay. I decided to work with a manager who was not supportive and later became antagonistic and hostile. It seemed that my escape from the first bank in Atlanta only served to transfer the test to another bank in Atlanta. I wondered, is it me? But it couldn't be me, I had worked in the industry for many years and I held the highest certification in the industry. Also, I had held long term positions and always got along well with everyone. It could not be me. My moving from New York to Atlanta, Georgia was much more significant to my life than I thought; it was more than a job relocation.

The only other thing in my life beside the Lord that I counted on was my career in Corporate Trust. I loved my profession, it had been an avenue of God's blessings and I genuinely enjoyed the work. The thought of changing professions never entered my mind, I was satisfied. After all, God had already done abundantly above anything that I could have ever asked or thought; I thought that He was satisfied too and that I had "arrived."

The Corporate Trust industry was beginning to undergo some changes, especially where I worked in

New York. I didn't particularly like the changes so I began to pray and ask God about my next direction. My thoughts were of moving to another bank in New York, I never considered a location outside of New York, but the Lord led me to the book of Joshua and I read it repeatedly, meditated in the book but I never got the revelation. Giants in the land! I did recognize the promise land (the relocation to Atlanta) but I didn't anticipate the giants!

Transitions can be difficult and I had no idea when I accepted the job relocation offer what God was up to, all I knew was that I believed the transfer was the leading of the Lord. I had been praying about the changes that were coming in the New York office and when I was asked if I would consider moving to Atlanta to work in the new office, I knew that this was the answer to my prayers. Later it was further confirmed that this was the answer to my prayers.

I knew that Atlanta was where I was supposed to be after all it was the direction that I had received from the Lord. I didn't know why specifically I was supposed to be in Atlanta but I was willing to relocate.

> "And Thou shalt remember all the way Which the Lord thy God lead thee these forty years in the wilderness, to humble thee, and to prove thee, to know what was in thine heart, whether thou wouldest keep His commandments or no."
> ~Deuteronomy 8; 2

It seemed that New Yorkers had special challenges within the industry in Atlanta, a preconceived notion that we thought we were better than everyone else, which to me seemed like nonsense but prejudice usually always exist in ways that don't make sense.

I knew it wasn't anything that I had done because a friend of mine had also accepted a position in Atlanta and moved from New York the year before I did, she took a Corporate Trust position in another Atlanta bank and also had similar problems. She eventually resigned her position at the bank and took a position with one of her clients. She often complained to me about how she was treated.

There was little to no opportunity for me in my profession in Atlanta but I believed that Atlanta was where I was supposed to be and if it was not, I expected God to tell me so. I expected that if He wanted to move me somewhere else including back to New York, He would let me know.

I stayed in my position and tried to work in an impossible situation. As I said, my manager had a reputation for eliminating people; getting rid of anyone who got in her way (which could be anyone depending on her mood). My predecessor, the woman that I was hired to replace, resigned and moved to the bank that I had left. I found out that there were others who had moved on before her, they relocated elsewhere. But rather than leaving, I decided to stay and fight, I rationalized that I had done nothing wrong and that God would protect me. My belief was that I was being discriminated against and that I had rights.

> "Your problem is not your problem. Your attitude - how you handle your problem – is your problem" ~John C. Maxwell

My manager was an expert at casting blame, I decided to clear myself of all false accusations and contrary to everything that I knew about existing in Corporate America, I eventually involved human resources in the situation. In the past I had counseled others not to do so (human resources is paid by the employer not the employee, so the loyalty may not be there, it depends on the company). It's always best to resolve the problem without their involvement if possible. Reasonable people can usually resolve problems through communication with one another but my manager was not a reasonable person. I never displayed any outward signs of anger with my manager; I smiled and tried to maintain as good a working relationship with her as possible, I continued to comply with her request even when they were ridiculous. On the outside I tried to be a good employee but inside I was angry and miserable.

Through the years, I had worked very hard to make it to where I was in my profession. Now, I worked for a person who wanted to take it away and for what, because of her own insecurities. Perhaps, if I had not given so much of myself to my profession, this would not have been such a disappointment. I had done everything to ensure that my place within the industry was secure and that I could move up within the industry. I believed that if I were going to remain in Atlanta, keeping this job was necessary.

> *"Deliver me from mine enemies, O my God; defend me from them that rise up against me"* ~Psalm 59; 1

Once when I was in my office, I laid my head on my desk and asked God, "Father has the brook dried up?" Thinking about Elijah in I Kings 17:7. It seemed that on some days everything that could go wrong did go wrong. In the financial services industry having a manager that is not supportive makes doing your job difficult. There are things within the financial services industry that can happen in the course of doing the job that can go either way depending on how the manager wants to handle it and my manager was after my head.

My every transaction became a potential notch in my manager's belt, so I had to as they say "cross my T's and dot my I's" to maintain a position that I saw as a blessing from God and the culmination of years of hard work. When others made mistakes or had issues my manager did what she called "damage control," I was never afforded that luxury. Any problem on any one of my accounts was magnified and I was reprimanded even if the situation was out of my control.

> *"And it came to pass after a while, that the brook dried up, because there had been no rain in the land"* ~ *I Kings 17:7*

I was emotionally tired and physically ill because of the length of time and intensity of the harassment. I needed to get out of there but I was too stubborn to take a leave of absence and quitting was not an option. It wasn't until the Encounter that I gave myself a break. I wanted God to show up like Superman and save me from the evil villain (my manager) and then fly away so that I could continue on with my life as usual. But God had different plans, He used the opportunity to help me develop and grow in my walk with Him. God may not have caused the situation but He did use the situation.

When I prayed prayers of consecration and dedication I didn't recognize the difficulties as an answer to my prayer. I thought that my life would get easier and that there were no difficulties in the faith walk. I thought that I could pray or positively confess the difficulties away. After thinking about what I'd been taught during the years, I realized I had not been taught that at all. Somewhere along the way I had assumed that there were no difficulties in the life of faith but that was not the message at all.

I never placed myself in the shoes of Peter, Paul or Jesus and others in the bible that got into difficulties although that is what I was supposed to do. It seemed to me that I had never heard anyone discuss problems on their job, everyone at church seemed perfect. For many years my concentration was on the victory and not on the opposition: to have a testimony there must be a test. To be an overcomer, there must be something to overcome.

> *"In the middle of difficulty lies opportunity". ~Albert Einstein*

I knew that God was with me but what I didn't think of at the time was that none of what I was going through was taking God by surprise. This entire situation was about my growth and destiny. I always thought that I would retire from my profession and I knew that I probably would not have left New York if I'd known that my Corporate Trust career would end in Atlanta.

Years before when I entered the financial services industry in Corporate Trust, I thought it was a perfect career for me; it was difficult for me to imagine a future without it. I didn't know that Atlanta was going to be a place of testing and proving of loss and renewal. In order for me to change direction, I had to be brought to a place of total trust and dependence on God.

Growing Pains

I know that God observes and watches over us attentively, He ordains and permits the times of our lives. He is always taking notice of us to see what we will do. That can seem strange considering that God knows everything, he is omnipresent and omnipotent. He already knows the outcome even before the event takes place.

But, I know that God allows us to make our decisions and our choices as a wise parent does with a growing child. It is important to Him that we know that our decisions and our ability to make wise decisions are important to Him. More specifically, our ability to make kingdom decisions based on His word and not on the world's influence, emotions and past experiences. I had spent seventeen years in Corporate America, I didn't want to leave, I wanted to stay and remain in the familiar. But my life was about to change. The Encounter prepared me for what I had to face when I returned to the office that day.

It may sound strange but I remember the joy that I felt as I entered the boardroom that day in September, the Encounter had put everything into perspective, I could have faced anything. I had used the time on the Encounter wisely; I had faced God and myself. I no longer felt the need to defend myself, I had repented for my actions and I was prepared to face my accuser and to meet my fate. The meeting was not difficult nor was it long. It was clear that the decision had already been made.

As I sat there listening to the comments being made, the seventeen years that I had spent in the industry went through my mind. From the battle to get off of welfare, my determination to attend and complete college after being out of school for so many years, the time spent away from my children while I tried to make a better life for us, it had been hard and now I was a Vice President and a specialist in my field.

I had mentored others during the years that were now in official positions themselves that gave me a great deal of satisfaction. I thought about the people in the boardroom and on the phone, people who had sought out my advice in the past and had thanked me for it. Although, I did not fully understand what God had in mind, I could feel His presence with me. I sat and quietly listened without any comment. It seems strange but I felt insulated, protected from the lies although my manager made sure that I would feel embarrassed, I didn't feel embarrassed at all; all I felt was peace.

> "What lies behind us and what lies before us are tiny matters compared to what lies within us" ~Walt Emerson

As I left the meeting, I was not angry; I had been prepared through the activities the weekend before at the Encounter and now it was over. I had faced it with faith, dignity, strength, and courage. I left there believing that this was not an end but a beginning. Mostly what was on my mind was a sense of "what now" the last time that I asked God that question, was when I became a Vice President, and when He answered, I thought that this new skill was to enhance my Corporate Trust career not to begin a new career!

Although I believed that God was in control, I realized that I didn't exactly know what that meant anymore, what just happened was not supposed to happen. In my mind, I wondered why my prayers had not been answered. I was at a place in my life where I had never been before; this meant a significant loss of income. I had just purchased a new house and taken on additional responsibility and care for an elderly parent and other family members, my family depended on my income. I had more questions than answers.

It immediately became apparent to me that I had to totally trust and rely on God not only for me but also for them. It felt uncomfortable like someone walking on a tight rope without a net. I learned that trust sounds nice in a Sunday morning sermon but the reality feels very different. Walking by faith is wonderful to learn about but the proof is in the doing, at first the feeling was somewhat unnerving. The enemy came immediately to remind me about how hard it had been to get off of welfare only to lose everything but I ignored him, he is a liar.

> "Are not two sparrows sold for a farthing? And one of them shall not fall on the ground without your Father. But the very hairs of your head are all numbered. Fear ye not therefore, ye are of more value than many sparrows" ~Matthew 10:29-31

I was a workaholic and now I had no job. I was in Atlanta, Georgia, not a financial center where a Corporate Trust job would be easy for me to come by. I wanted to hear God say "go back to New York" but I didn't hear that. I didn't like the feeling of losing my job, especially under these circumstances. My paper work said resignation but you don't qualify for unemployment when you resign, I received unemployment and I also received a separation package. It was handled by Human Resources for obvious reasons.

The Human Resources specialist told me privately that basically it came down to a personality conflict. She also said that my manager had done several wrong things and that she would be undergoing training in conflict resolution. Considering that I was the one without a job her words were not comforting. It was obvious that they knew that I was not the problem. It was obvious that this was not the first time that they had problems with this manager. All I could guess from our interaction was that my manager had support from someone very high in the organization and nothing was going to change.

I didn't know how soon I would get another job or what type of job it would be. I was determined to do whatever God told me to do, I was totally out of my comfort zone and all I could do now was to trust Him to make this right.

> "The steps of a good man are ordered by the Lord: and he delighteth in his way. Though he fall, he shall not be utterly cast down: for the Lord upholdeth him with His hand" ~Psalm 37; 23-24

I remember the drive home after being escorted out of my office by my manager and co-worker, a black woman who had acted as a buffer to protect my manager from any appearance of discrimination. I remember embracing each of them with a hug and saying goodbye, I had worked with them for three years and although I didn't like what they had done, I didn't want to leave in anger or un-forgiveness.

During the drive home I reminded God that I had a solid court case, everything was documented, and I had been discriminated against, harassed, isolated and treated unfairly. I knew that unfair labor practices had been committed but I wanted to focus more on my spiritual wellbeing. I told God "they lied on me" and He said "they lied on me too, let it go." Those words made me realized that all the time that I had spent gathering evidence could have been more wisely spent in prayer and in the Word. This was not about them; it was about God, me and our relationship. It was about timing and purpose. At that point, I relaxed; I let it go and allowed the peace of God and the comfort of the Holy Spirit to begin a work in me.

Abba Father

There is no denying the love of God, while at times during this trial I felt alone there was never a time when I really was, God was with me all the time. He dealt with me based on His love for me. When I think about God, I see Him as my father and as my father; I know that He wants the best for me. That knowledge kept me through some very difficult times in the months and years that followed. I had been taught that God never ends anything on a negative, and that man's idea of failure is many times God's idea of promotion, so I decided to pursue God's new direction for my life as soon as I knew what it was.

> "A successful man is one who can lay a firm foundation with the bricks others have thrown at him". ~David Brinkley

Like most parents, God chose to exercise His right to teach me through the difficulty. Although His choice for me at the time seemed hard, I realize now that God knew more about my destiny than I did. I decided to get to know this aspect of God's character by experiencing it not only in theory but also in practice.

When my life was going smoothly and I had all that I needed, I had taken Him for granted; I attended church, served in church, prayed, praised and worshipped but there were still areas inside of me that were hidden, blind spots. When my personal belief system was challenged, these blind spots were exposed. When I was under pressure and stretched beyond the usual limits, I began to see the problems myself. God, like most fathers gives correction but like most children, I had no desire to be corrected. Still, as a parent myself, I realize that sometimes discipline is necessary and is always good when it's done in love.

I knew that I had become too familiar with God. I was at a place in my spiritual growth where I could not assume that God would agree with everything that I did. After all, I was supposed to be in step with Him and not the other way around. The situation can be compared to that of a child whose level of responsibility increases when they become a teenager. My level of responsibility to God had increased but I was too busy to recognize it. As a parent, I understand that it is my responsibility to help my children develop into mature adults who I hope will emulate the character and behavior that they have seen modeled. Just like a natural parent, God had to remind me that He cared about the person that I was becoming and not what my job or my title was. My actions had sown seeds and some of them had to be reaped, God continued to love me and teach me through the difficult times.

> "Be not deceived God is not mocked: for whatsoever a man soweth, that shall he also reap" ~Galatians 6; 7

A time of testing can expose imperfections; scars of the past, all of the flaws that are hidden at other times. I learned how to trust and totally rely on God. I learned about integrity, submission, faith and purpose, not as the world defines it but as the Kingdom defines it. I thought that I had all of these areas in my life covered before but I found that everything has levels and depths.

I knew that I had to humble myself and allow God to reveal what needed to be revealed and to help me to make the changes that needed to be made. I had made changes in life before but they were deliberate, this was thrust upon me and I had very few answers and a lot of questions.

> "My brethren, count it all joy when ye fall into divers temptations knowing this that the trying of your faith worketh patience But let patience have her perfect work, that ye may be perfect and entire wanting nothing" ~James 1:2-4

In this scripture what is being tried is the faith not the patience but patience is increased because God's timing is different from our timing. I had to believe that God would help me to glean all of the information out of this situation that He would continue to help me to make it through the process. I knew that the perfection of my character was His ultimate goal and I knew that the enemy was out to destroy me in any way that he could. My responsibility was to learn and develop through this crisis and since I had time now to spend in His presence in a way that I hadn't in a long time, I resolved to do just that.

I decided to pursue a level of intimacy with God that can't be reached when emotional walls are up and when the fast pace of life serves to keep your relationship on a superficial basis. I knew that pride and stubbornness had brought about this crisis but I also knew that crisis was a doorway which I had to walk through. Regardless of why or how the crisis came, I knew that when I began to relate to God, He would begin to reveal to me what His direction for me was. I was determined to remain appreciative realizing that He was the potter and that I was the clay

CHAPTER 2

Looking Back Can Be Good

I Want you to come and go with me on the journey that I had to take. My hope is that you will recognize some of the strategies and road blocks that the enemy may set before you on your journey. I want to be as transparent as possible about some of the things that I experienced and allow you to see me in a vulnerable state. I'd like you to see the faithfulness of God and to know that no matter where you are, He is there with you. Each of us will encounter challenges on our individual journeys in life, our testimonies are important. Our testimonies are not only a witness to the lost, but they are a source of information and encouragement to other believers. It is important that we humble ourselves enough to look at the experiences of others without being critical or judgmental and acknowledge that "there but by the grace of God go I."

Each of us has an assignment in this earth realm and many times by the time that we reach adulthood, pitfalls and obstacles have already been placed in our path to hinder us from reaching our purpose. Neglect, abuse, rejection are a few things that are designed to keep us from reaching our destiny. Sometimes in order for us to move forward we have to review the past and come to terms with the areas in our lives that are deeply buried beneath emotional baggage or walls. These walls may have been originally erected for protection but have since become barriers, not letting others in but also not letting you out. These things have no place in the life of a citizen of the Kingdom of God.

Unfortunately, the enemy does not forget the events and tragedies that have shaped our past; the things that we have chosen to bury and to forget. Those buried, forgotten areas are what the enemy uses to impede our progress toward a specific goal. Some people call these obstacles roadblocks, setbacks, strongholds or stuck places. We must confront these places within ourselves before we can enter into the deeper things that God has for us. Also, it is important to remember that the devil is a thief; he comes to steal, kill, and destroy. Two of the things that the enemy wants to steal from you is your testimony, and your vision.

When we are ignorant of the devils devices and subtleties we can be caught unaware like a deer in the headlights of an oncoming car. To further complicate matters, when we consider ourselves "mature" Christians," we can become too sure of ourselves in many ways and the enemy will give us a false sense of well-being. When the enemy attacks, he doesn't use the things that are obvious to us like things that we might consider "major sin." Satan does not come with the obvious but will use the less obvious the obscure doorway into your life.

Satan uses the hidden things; hurts and abuses, these hurts may be generational a result of iniquity. He uses areas that are hidden below the surface. These are also the areas that God wants to reveal and heal but some of these things can only be changed when they are made manifest to us. The enemy is so subtle that if you are not aware, your mind and mouth can be the instruments that are used against you. For instance, if at any time during the reading of this book you find yourself saying "she should have known better" remember the admonition in the Word about judging and remember that it's not about falling; it's about whether or not you get back up. The test and trials may come but the overcomer prevails and receives the spoils of battle. You can't receive the spoils without the battle.

> *"Judge not that you be not judged. For with the judgment ye judge ye shall be judged: and with the measure ye mete, it shall be measured to you again"* ~ Matthew 7; 1-2

In my own situation, God wanted me to slow down, but I wanted to speed up and Satan wanted to take me out. When my life came to a complete halt because of the abrupt end of my career after months of prayer and what

I thought at the time was "trusting God" I had to do some serious soul searching and reflecting.

A New Day

Entrances and exits in life are important, they hold a level of significance that must be scrutinized; I was taught to examine closely how I entered and how I left situations. The thought behind that teaching was that however you exit one situation will determine how you enter the next. For example, people who experience divorce can take many of the hurts that they have suffered in the first relationship into the next relationship; especially if they don't allow themselves the time needed for healing. Since my last position had ended badly, I wanted to make sure that I held no unforgiveness in my heart toward anyone; I wanted to be careful not to take any emotional baggage from that situation into my next position or into my life. I didn't know when I would get the opportunity to begin working again but I fully expected that it would be soon.

> *"Others can stop you temporarily, but you're the only one who can do it permanently" ~John C. Maxwell*

I had a lot of questions for God. During the situation at work, I had prayed to God so many times about what was going on and I believed that God would intervene. It was my hope that everything would eventually be worked out between my manager and me and that we would arrive at a workable solution. I didn't think that God might have some ideas of His own about the situation, my future, or how this situation would end.

> *"Therefore I will look unto the Lord; I will wait for the God of my salvation: my God will hear me. When I sit in darkness, the Lord shall be a light unto me"~ Micah 7:7-8*

Leaving the bank was a good thing for me because the pressure and stress had begun to take its toll. Regardless of what was said, I knew that I had made a positive contribution to the bank and that some of the things that were accomplished was a direct result of my being there. But as the saying goes "you will only be remembered for two things in life, the problems that you solve or the ones that you create" and most people have selective memory, they remember what they want to remember.

Not long after I left the bank, I learned that four other people (including the remaining two vice presidents, (one of which was the black female who acted as a buffer for my manager) also left. They left all together at once and joined a competitor bank. After they left, only five junior people remained to administer a full load of Corporate Trust accounts which they had no experience with.

After that, the Corporate Trust business of the bank was acquired by the bank that I worked for in New York, the bank that had relocated me to Atlanta. This was the same Corporate Trust bank where the woman who I was hired to replace had found a job when she left the bank to get away from my ex-manager. She was now the manager of that Corporate Trust business. Many of the original people were no longer there. She was now in a position equal to the person who had harassed her and caused her to leave her position. The bank decided to choose between the two managers, I'm not sure why they decided to do it this way. I had worked in many mergers and acquisitions including for this bank and they usually maintained their manager. But for some reason and because a choice had to be made between the two existing managers, rather than work with my ex-manager again, this woman took a buy-out package and left the bank. My ex-manager was now the new manager. What a strange course of events.

I could have stayed at the first bank because that entire staff turned over after I left. The bank that I moved to was now acquired by the bank that I left. I realized that had I stayed put, my situation would have been entirely different.

I believed that it was important for me to examine what had gone wrong in my situation, so I decided to look back and take a life inventory. I wanted to remember and examine what made me the person I had come to be. Because I had undergone a major life shift, I needed to give it some perspective. It had been a very long time since I had given my past any thought at all. I had bought into a philosophy that said I should not look back but now, I knew that the philosophy was better interpreted as "don't dwell on the past." But now I know you can reflect on the past, focus on the present and imagine the future. When I looked back I saw how very far I had come, I was no longer the person I was when I started out. Every aspect of my life had changed.

Perception and reality

To perceive is to become aware of directly through the senses, to take notice of by observation. My manager had observed me and apparently didn't like what she saw or perhaps she saw more in me than she was comfortable seeing. All I wanted was to do my job and to maintain the lifestyle that I had become accustomed to. At the time, I was very content with the status quo. But I'm always learning and improving. Maybe I was perceived as being competitive. My intentions however were never to compete with my manager. I didn't want to become stagnant so I took every growth opportunity that came my way. I believe in personal growth and development.

There were times when my ex-manager diverted the more lucrative and interesting accounts from me and gave them to one of my colleagues. She would shift less lucrative and drudge work assignments my way. It became boring for me. I did the work but, I also participated in other activities within the bank to keep my skills sharp. I was aware of the tactics that my ex-manager was using. I'd seen her use the same tactics on others.

My main strength had always been my ability to work independently on assignments and to make good decisions without exceeding my authority. But, my ex-manager perceived this strength as aggression or overreaching, it was a source of irritation to her. She tried to block my progress but at every opportunity, I navigated around the block. I followed one opportunity and was given a seat on the bank's Capital Market's Diversity Counsel. My role on the Counsel gave me a high level of visibility within the bank. This was another source of irritation for her but at the time I was not being competitive, I was improving myself.

The Counsel met monthly in Charlotte, North Carolina. At first, my manager insisted that I drive to Charlotte, North Carolina from Atlanta, Georgia for the meeting but, when I told the Executive Vice President that I was asked to drive rather than fly, he insisted that I fly and use his cost center to pick up the expense.

I was able to fly to Charlotte every month for the seventeen months that I served on the Counsel until I left the bank. I served on the Counsel with senior management and others in the Capital Markets Group. Also on the Counsel was my ex-manager's boss, and his boss, they were Senior and Executive Vice Presidents. My membership on the Counsel gave me the ability to work on several important and successful projects for the bank. So although my boss tried to block me, it was her actions with my accounts that gave me the time to actually serve on the Counsel. Even in a time of adversity God caused me to excel.

> "And it came to pass as they came, when David was returned from the slaughter of the Philistine that the women came out of all cities of Israel, singing and dancing to meet King Saul, with tabrets, with joy, and with instruments of music. And the women answered one another as they played and said "Saul has slain his thousands and David his ten thousands" and Saul was very wroth, and the saying displeased him; and he said, "they have ascribed unto David ten thousand, and to me they have ascribed but thousands: and what can he have more but the kingdom?" ~I Samuel 18: 6-8

The time that I spent serving on the Diversity Counsel was an amazing time. I didn't realize it at the time but I had already begun to move into my future. The networking and the projects that I worked on with my team gave me a platform to do presentations and to have a voice in the direction that the bank was moving in toward diversity. It was a team effort something that I was not experiencing in my office in Atlanta. As I reflect back on my experience in the Counsel, my memories are happy memories and I am aware that it was a breath of fresh air during a very difficult time.

I still wrestled with my job loss, I questioned, was racism a factor? Was jealousy a factor? I don't really know. What I began to realize was that there was nothing that I could do about it. I realized that the only person that I had control over in the situation was me. I realized that in order for me to move forward I needed to take one hundred percent responsibility for me and to never give up my personal power. God says that "He will perfect that which concerneth me." I knew that God had taken me from the bottom before and He could do it again. The first thing that I did when I left the bank was to get some rest; I decided to look back over my life and to take inventory of my past. I knew that my future depended upon me becoming the person that God intended for me to be. I believed that something good was going to come out of this situation. I also decided to think more seriously about the Word that God had given me. Along the way God said things to me that didn't make any sense. God told me that I needed a professional headshot so I found a photographer and had a headshot done. I didn't know why I needed a headshot at the time; I used it in a mailing to my Corporate Trust clients because I could only see myself within my current profession. It wasn't until I published my first book in 2005 and the publisher said "you need a headshot" that it clicked! God is amazing.

> *"It's not whether you get knocked down; it's whether you get up"* ~Vince Lombardi

The problem with things that disrupt your life is that they seldom are expected and they seldom make a clean break. I had two immediate needs: I needed a job, and I needed to know what God had planned for me because I didn't have anything planned for myself. I had put everything I had into my career. At the time that I received the Word from the Lord, I didn't understand it; I thought it had something to do with banking, with Corporate Trust. But even prior to leaving the bank, I began to think about it more and more. I had to get a better understanding of who I was and why I had been brought to this crossroad.

Looking Back

I began the look back into my past at the very beginning, my childhood. I didn't want to leave any area unexplored that the enemy could use later. My earliest memories were of growing up in my grandparent's home in Washington D.C.; I was the youngest child in the immediate family. I enjoyed most of my childhood but I didn't understand why I lived with my grandparents. I realized that living with my grandparents provided me with the stability that I needed to make it through some of the tough times that I would experience later in my life. My grandparents financial, emotional and physical stability contributed to my overall wellbeing and I was grateful to God for that but there was always a sense of something missing.

My grandmother was a Bishop in our Pentecostal church, she was strict and she had some very specific expectations for us which were: (1) Love God, (2) Get an education and (3) work hard.

Growing up as a Pentecostal, I spent a lot of time in church. In church I learned church doctrine and bible stories, I enjoyed Sunday school lessons and sermons, I enjoyed singing in the choir, but what I remember most was the long list of things that we could not do. As I remembered my childhood, I realized that I had also been taught a set of core values which were not always based on the bible, some were based on tradition, history and ethnicity.

My generation went through a lot growing up. We grew up in a time of dramatic changes and many changing ideologies. The Vietnam war, Watergate, Presidential and Civil Rights Leader's assassinations, the Civil Rights Movement, segregation, the Black Panther Party, the hippie era, free love, drug culture, and more television and advertising than any previous generation. We were imprinted with a need to embrace the "new."

My generation is a critical generation but, we dropped the ball. We were rebellious in many ways and some of the effects of our rebellion are still being realized today. Even now, in this situation, the rebellion that was in me made me vulnerable.

> *"I may not be able to change the world I see around me, but I can change the way I see the world within me"* ~ Unknown

As I reflected more on my past I noticed a pattern, I began to believe the Word that the Lord had given me. I recalled the training and development that I received as a child; I recalled the popularity and influence that I enjoyed during high school, the leadership roles that I held in high school: senior class president, cosmetology shop president a co-captain of the Girl's Drill Team.

From testifying and singing in church to delivering the welcome address at my high school graduation, I was always in front of people speaking. I began to see that I had always held leadership roles and influence even as a teen. Glimpses of my future were all over my past but I had pushed it aside to remain in my comfort zone.

> "Great things are not done by impulse but by a series of small things brought together"~ Unknown

I recalled that as our family dined nightly together; after my cousin and I helped my grandmother prepared dinner and set the table. My grandfather always blessed the food before we ate and then my grandparents would tell us stories about our family, these stories gave me a profound sense of history. We always had interesting conversations during dinner.

My grandparents were hardworking individuals and life had not always been easy for them but by the time they took on the responsibility for raising me and my cousin, they were financially comfortable. It would be fair to say that we were middle class. My grandfather worked for the railroad and also had his own business. Although he gave my grandmother a nice allowance, she earned additional money by producing various arts and crafts; she was very creative and extremely industrious, an entrepreneur at heart and she was a very independent thinker. She loved making things and teaching us how to make things too.

While we ate dinner, my grandparents often talked about Dr. Meyers our great uncle who was a friend of Marcus Garvey, Dr. Meyers was a teacher, minister, published author and a scholar. He married Flora Toole Meyers; she graduated from college at the age of sixteen.

They talked about Sam Toole, my great grandfather and about his wife Georgiana McMillan Toole, my great-grandmother, how we could trace her family history back using a document that we called the scroll, which was a notarized copy of a page from the family bible that my great grandmother had copied, notarized and distributed to the family before the family bible was destroyed. They talked about the Meyer's Industrial High School, 806 Payne St. in Knoxville, Tennessee, this was the colored school that our family owned and managed, they were all educators and ministers. They spoke of a time when our family was prominent in the Black and White communities in Tennessee and were property owners and well respected.

I didn't understand it all as a child but as an adolescent, I began to realize that my friends didn't have similar family histories and I began to appreciate the stories more. The pictures and the old documents we had gave the stories more meaning and credibility. The stories gave me a sense of ancestral pride. But, like most families there was another side to our family too. Some of the history was not good and caused division and strife within the family.

Because my grandfather worked for the railroad, we were able to travel by train throughout the United States. My grandmother also liked taking cross country driving road trips. We had a house in Washington D.C. and a summer home in Whitesboro, New Jersey where we spent the summer months. When I reached junior high school, we didn't travel as much instead we spent our entire summers in South New Jersey. It was fun being at the shore.

My grandmother believed in hard work, so we worked during the entire summer months too. I had a job even when I was too young to get working papers. I have had some type of job as long as I can remember. By my second year of high school, I was already a licensed Manicurist and the following year I worked as an apprentice in a local beauty salon in Washington D.C. I was a shampoo person but I learned a lot about being a hair stylist as well. I attended a Vocational High School and became a licensed cosmetologist before my high school graduation. I worked for several years; working for such notable salons as "Soul Scissors" in the 70's Soul Scissors was a premier Black Hair Care Salon, the first of its kind. The salon was extremely popular.

I worked in that profession on and off for about thirteen years. When I moved to New York, I was employed with Soul Scissors in Washington, DC; it was their first salon on the east coast. Soul Scissors was originally from Los Angeles, California. When they opened their second salon on the east coast in Jamaica Queens, NY, I relocated to New York. I lost my job when I got pregnant. Being young, I did not know to inquire about company benefits when I got morning sickness that prevented me from arriving to work. My subway ride from Harlem to Queens was spent between the subway cars throwing up. There was no one in my life at the time that could counsel or advise me based on my work history and background and I was young and clueless.

I had always worked but now that I could not work I needed advice. When I sought advice from my family and friends in Harlem, my current environment, I was introduced to the Welfare system. I followed their advice. This introduced me to a life of dependency. When my son was a year old, I went back to work, off and on. Two years later I had my daughter, I, like many others around me, remained connected to the system. Some of the people around me had always been on welfare.

Because I had a skill, I could always work off and on and I did. And, because of my up-bringing, I knew that there was a better way. Eventually, the dissatisfaction within me and the desire for a better life prompted me to attend college.

I don't believe that it is an accident that many of the stories in the bible begin with genealogies; the Hebrews understood that it was important to remember the past. I will always be grateful to my grandparents for their diligence in my upbringing. The genealogy that they continued to share with us daily reinforced in me that I should be self-sufficient and not rely on someone else like welfare. My family history contributed significantly to who I am and why I believe that I could overcome any obstacle.

When we don't deal with the issues within our past by acknowledging them before God and seeking His healing, the enemy can use our past against our future. What I realized about my past was that because of my upbringing, I was very strong mentally and I never felt inferior or ill equipped to handle my manager's tactics. Yes, I resented her tactics but now after some reflecting, I realized that she had not only insulted my present, she had insulted my past and although I knew what the Word of God said on the subject, my core values learned from my family were stronger than the Word of God in me when it came to how I used my personal strength.

The enemy knew that I was not going to allow someone to label me or to hold me back. The enemy also knew that I would not give up so easily or quit. Not giving up or quitting in this situation was not good, it was the area that allowed the enemy entrance because the only thing that could have turned things around was for me to humble myself and to truly surrender to God and to trust Him. Truthfully, at the time, I thought that I had surrendered to God. I thought that I was trusting in Him but now I realize that I really had not fully surrendered to God. I relied a lot on my mind and not my spirit. It reminded me of a statement that Jesus made related to this in John 14:30.

> *"Hereafter I will not talk much with you: for the prince of this world cometh, and hath nothing in me"* ~John 14:30

Jesus is saying that there is nothing that is in Him that Satan can use against Him or as it says in the Message Bible "no claim on Him." If you can imagine what Jesus must have gone through as a child of questionable birth by a woman who claimed to be a virgin, how many people do you think believed that Mary was a virgin or that God was Jesus father? I'm sure that there were whispers from people around Him. Once during a conversation with Jesus the Pharisees said to Him "We be not born of fornication." Why do you think that they replied to Him in that way? But while Jesus never allowed anyone else to define Him, He also never became offended by what others said or did. He never gave the enemy an opportunity or place in Him. While He would display righteous indignation, He never became offended. Righteous indignation is anger due to the mistreatment, insult, or malice of another but offense is a condition of the individual's heart.

> *"Ye do the deeds of your father. Then said they to Him, we be not born of fornication; we have one father, even God"* ~John 8:41

As I reflected on each decade of my life each memory helped me to see the pattern that had shaped me. Like most teens, I enjoyed dancing, movies and friends but it seemed that there was always something missing. I loved music, singing, reading and drawing. I was caught up in the politics and style of the times. My hair reflected it, my clothes reflected it and so did my conversation. Much of what I knew about what I called "real Life" came from the television and the movies of the time.

Like most teenagers, I believed that I knew everything; I didn't think that my grandparents had a clue about anything. I was very immature and much too sheltered and spoiled, but because I didn't live with my parents I don't think that I felt loved. My immaturity made me fertile ground for adopting the wrong influence, ideas, and people. When the hair salon that I worked in opened a shop in New York, I did the one thing that I had planned to do all of my life, I moved to New York because my mother was there.

""Every change in human attitude must come through internal understanding and acceptance. Man is the only known creature who can reshape and remold himself by altering his attitude" ~John C. Maxwell

After a period of time in New York, I was jobless, penniless and pregnant. I was too embarrassed to call my grandparents so like many of the people on the block where I lived in New York; I applied for welfare and started receiving "my check." From that day until the day that I was hired on my first bank job, I was connected to the welfare system in some way. The welfare system creates a dependence that people who have never depended on it can understand. Many people who have been on the system think that they cannot make it without welfare. I knew that the ease of my transition off of welfare was due to the grace of God and the training and work ethic instilled in me by my grandparents.

After two failed relationships, two children and a lot of chaos in between, while working in a hair salon in the Wall Street area of New York City, something started to stir in me, a feeling of dissatisfaction and discontent. I started to ask my clients questions about where they worked and what they did. I decided to go to college. I never had a desire to attend college before but now I really wanted to attend so I applied for financial aid and received a college education. In college my writing gift began to emerge, I didn't know it at the time but God was calling me.

When God Calls

It was during the same period of time; my mother began to attend church and got saved or born again. It was funny in a way because we were studying a different ideology when this happened. My mother quickly began to try to get me converted too. Being raised as I was, this was not something at the time that I wanted to do but my mother would not stop witnessing to me.

I was still enjoying myself too much I thought; I practically lived at the disco. I liked to party. When I worked in the salon most of the staff was young and we regularly partied after work. It was common for us to go to the club and dance until it closed and then go to the after-hours spot. When we emerged from the after-hours spot, it was daylight. When we came out people were waiting at the bus stop dressed in their Sunday best on their way to church.

When I finally arrived home, still unable to sleep, I would turn on the television. On Sunday mornings most of the programming was religious. I especially liked to watch Fred KC Price broadcast "Ever Increasing Faith." I knew enough of the Word from my upbringing to know that he knew what he was talking about. The way He taught was compelling and confrontational, it reminded me of what the people said about Jesus in the bible, he taught with authority. He did not sugar coat the Word, he gave it to you straight, and I liked watching his broadcast.

One day while planning my birthday party with a friend at a local bar, in my spirit I heard the voice of God say "it's time." I was literally sitting on a bar stool making party plans when I said to God in my spirit "I know, but not now, I will come to you after the party." We had the party but it didn't go as planned; it was not a good party at all. I guess that was God's way of paying me back for putting Him on hold, God does have a sense of humor.

My mother continued to pray for me and God was still arranging things because a month after the party my favorite television preacher came to New York! Yes, Frederick K.C. Price of Crenshaw Christian Center and the television show, Ever Increasing Faith was coming. We attended his meeting at the Nassau Coliseum and I gave my life to Jesus Christ, I was baptized in the Holy Spirit with the bible evidence of speaking in tongues the same night and I was instantly delivered from a lot of things.

God was so good; He saved my best friend in about a month. We began to attend church as much as we used to attend the club. We had a sincere desire to know the Word of God so we often read and studied the bible together. We could not get enough of the word. We joined a church and my life did a 180 degree turn; I never looked back.

A New Direction

Looking back, I remembered participating in "New York Works," the welfare to work program that I attended while also attending college, I remembered my first bank job interview. I was so happy when I got my first bank job because it meant that we could move to a better neighborhood. My son was already showing the signs of the effects of the environment that we lived in and I knew that I had to move to save him from the environment. We lived in a neighborhood in Staten Island, NY known as Parkhill (sometimes referred to as "Killahill" or "Shaolin"). We needed to move badly. I remembered graduating college with a bachelor's degree thinking that now I would get a raise in pay on my job.

When I got my first bank job I did not know the rules of Corporate America so I followed the advice of Mr. Bertram Wallace, one of the instructors at New York Works. Mr. Wallace told us "you have got to bite the bullet and smile." I enjoyed reading; I read self-help books as well as my bible. I paid close attention to how the officers in the bank where I worked dressed, how they talked, and how they carried themselves; I began to emulate every successful and admired officer in the bank.

I didn't realize that what I was doing was exercising a spiritual principle-You have to see yourself where you want to be long before you arrive there, I just wanted to do a good job. All of my actions were eventually rewarded.

> *"For as he thinketh in his heart so is he..."~Proverbs 23:7*

In my first Corporate Trust position I was selected for special assignments which enhanced my resume. I eventually moved from the operations department into the administration department, this was considered difficult to do because believe it or not, even then, the operations department was predominately Black, while the administration department was predominately White with a few Hispanics. I was hired into the asset backed finance group which was the premier group within Corporate Trust at that time. I soaked up every bit of knowledge that I could. Even then God helped me.

A couple of things let me know that I was not going to stay at the very first bank where I worked; number one; when I took my college degree to human resources they said that I was not entitled to a raise or a promotion because I was now a college graduate (I had the job before I graduated college). And number two; when it was time for a promotion, I didn't get one. Although, when my immediate supervisor had left the bank months earlier and was not immediately replaced, I covered her duties and mine.

Number three; people kept telling me not to learn things, they would say "You will never need to know this so you don't need to learn about it" even then I knew that knowledge was power, especially in that environment. I not only wanted to know how, I wanted to know why because I had learned that the man who knows how will always have a job but the man who knows why will always be his boss.

> *"Progress is a tide. If we stand still we will surely be drowned. To stay on the crest, we have to keep moving"* ~Harold Mayfield

This period was just before banks and trust companies started to acquire one another. It was the very beginning of the downsizing era. Downsizing made the banks lean enough to do mergers and acquisitions. My bank offered a voluntary separation package the first of its kind but not the last as the industry began to consolidate; it was a very generous package. It was not based on years of service or age; it was first come first serve. Whoever arrived first received the package. Some separation packages were as much as a full year's wages and others were more. The packages were so generous that some employees camped out overnight to get the package. I did not camp out overnight but I did arrive early enough to get a package, I worked four years at that bank before taking the package.

Each job that I accepted after that was a step up. I consulted for a period of time and gained some invaluable Corporate Trust experience. The knowledge that I gained while on those assignments helped me to get the promotions later in my career. At that time in New York each time an individual moved to another bank their salary increased, sometimes the increase was substantial. I remembered one experience that I had; I had an interview during my lunch hour with a bank and during that interview, I was offered an additional ten thousand dollars more per year; I told them that I would think about the offer. I returned to work and told my manager about the offer. My manager countered the offer, in other words, because someone else was willing to give me ten thousand dollars more per year, my manager said, "We don't want to lose you, we will give you the ten thousand dollars more per year and you don't have to leave."

This was a common practice in New York. I stayed where I was, which was good because the bank where I interviewed was soon acquired by another bank. The acquiring bank did not retain the employees of the department that had interviewed me. I would have been without a job. God's hand was evident, again.

"We are living in days of change. My grandfather had a farm. My father had a garden. But I've got a can opener" ~Unknown

Looking at my past was an exercise that I had to take. It helped me to deal with the enemy when he tried to torment me about the uncertainty of the future. I remembered that I had already been through some unbelievable experiences and that God had brought me through them all, this gave me the strength to endure. This was just a new type of challenge and this challenge would also eventually end.

Up to the time that I arrived in Georgia, my career made a steady upward progression. I knew that I had always been fair to others because as the saying goes "you meet the same people going up that you meet coming down." And if I had stayed in New York, I know that there would have been some friendly faces but in Georgia things were different. With the exception of my clients, some attorneys that I worked with, and some sympathetic others, the faces were not friendly. I guess that I had failed to fit in, or maybe I had broken too many unwritten rules and I admit that I was probably too different, like the peacock in the book "Peacock in the Land of the Penguins" I just didn't fit in.

After losing my job I had the time to start moving toward the Word that the Lord had given me. I didn't have the total vision, many things were still unclear but I began to act on the parts of the vision that were clear. I continued to struggle emotionally with the job loss and how my career had ended; I launched an intense job search while I also began to move toward my vision and dream.

After a period of time my lifestyle began to suffer. There is absolutely nothing like holding on to God's hand especially when there is no other hand to hold. Day after day I had to seek God for the basic necessities of life. The more I drew close to God the more He drew close to me. Whenever I didn't know what to do next, I would ask Him, and He would say "Press in" which I knew meant to continue to fast and pray, believe and trust Him.

During this time, in spite of all of the distractions, I was able to write and publish my first book. I didn't understand everything yet but I knew that it had to do with my relationship with God. Knowing that caused me to ask God "Who am I... really?" why was I under attack? Why had I encountered so much opposition? I wanted to know who God saw when He looked at me. What His thoughts toward me were.

Those questions could take me only one place, to His Word. I discovered that it was not only my pride that had caused the adversity but that there were other reasons why I was facing adversity. I saw people in the bible who had lost everything and who had undergone tragedy for various reasons.

In the book of Job, Job became a target of Satan because he was righteous. In the book of Jonah, Jonah was eaten by a great fish because of his disobedience. In the book of 2 Corinthians, Paul had a thorn in the flesh a messenger of Satan sent to buffet him lest he be exalted without measure. In the book of Acts, Stephen was stoned to death for telling the truth. In the book of Genesis, Joseph was sold into slavery by his brothers because of jealousy. In the book of Matthew, Jesus was lied on and betrayed for thirty pieces of silver. I was confident that if I humbled myself, that in His season, He would exalt me.

As I moved forward, each day seemed to get harder and harder, my flesh (my mind, will and emotions) did not like the hardship but my spirit flourished because God was the only one who I could lean on. The book writing projects allowed me to be productive doing something that I wanted to do (write) while doing something that I didn't want to do (look for a job). When I left the bank, I was given out placement services which included classes on interview technique, resume writing, etc., the out placement company had daily classes that I was required to attend.

The activity was supposed to help us to keep our corporate mindset, to help us to not miss going to work and to keep a productive attitude. Eventually, I had taken all of the classes that I could and I was placed on a team composed of others who were also still looking for a job.

The theory behind the team concept was accountability. The weekly meeting was a time that we came together to report on our week's activities; interviews, phone calls and potential interviews or networking activities, we gave weekly reports in the team meeting and passed on information which we may not have been able to use but that we believed another team member might find useful.

Each week we reported our job search efforts to one another. Everything was very detailed; there were special spreadsheets and websites and templates designed to aid us in our job search. We had special computer software and subscriptions to help us get to the hiring manager and the decision makers at our target company. We were assigned to a professional job search expert to assist our team. She coached us and tried to help us stay focused on the job search, she also provided encouragement. Many of the team members had been out of work for a long time, two to three years.

There was only one problem with the team, no one was getting hired. As I looked around the table one day I began to realize that we all had something in common everyone on the team was at the top of their field with credential and years of experience and we were all middle aged.

I worked a few one day temporary assignments but nothing that brought in much money. During that time we lived on unemployment and my savings. Finally I had to liquidate my 401K and sale some stock out of my stock portfolio. It was not easy to watch my retirement saving dwindle as I continued to pursue an unsuccessful job search. I continued to press forward.

CHAPTER 3

Introspection: Taking a Look Inside

After I'd spent a period of time reflecting on the past, I wanted to know how and if I had changed, if I'd changed at all. Certainly, such a tragic end to my career must have had an impact on me, so I directed my observations inward. I wanted to know what effect the people and events had on me. Had this experience left a mark on the person who I was?

After all, I had been so sure of myself, so confident and so professional. I needed to know if these unfortunate experiences had caused me to be unsure of myself. What had become a part of me because of this experience that I needed to deal with? I was sure that the emotional baggage of my past had contributed to the situation and I was determined that everything that needed to be resolved must to be resolved now; I would not take it into my future.

Moving forward, I knew that I had to make some changes, the changes had to be deliberate and desired; there was no time to waste feeling sorry for myself. I detest pity parties, I wasn't about to fall into that trap. Actually, I should say that I wouldn't stay there because momentary lapses had already occurred. Yes, there were times that I found myself saying "woe is me" but I knew from past experience that if I stayed there, with that attitude, I could not move forward and I wanted very much to move forward.

I knew that God had plans for me to become the person who He wanted me to be but I also realized that the responsibility for me to become that person was mine. Yes, God was willing to use even my mistakes to turn things around for my good but I also knew that if I had listened to Him better before, there would be no need for Him to rescue me now. I understood now better than ever what the Apostle Paul meant in the book of Romans when he wrote about the struggle that we go through in our flesh.

> *"Examine yourselves, whether ye be in the faith; prove your own selves. Know ye not your own selves, how that Jesus Christ is in you, except you be reprobate"~I Corinthians 13:5*

> *"For I know that in me (that is, in my flesh,) dwelleth no good thing: for to will is present with me; but how to perform that which is good I find not. For the good that I would I do not: but the evil which I would not, that I do. Now if I do that I would not, it is no more I that do it, but sin that dwelleth in me. I find then a law, that, when I would do good, evil is present with me. For I delight in the law of God after the inward man: But I see another law in my members, warring against the law of my mind, and bringing me into captivity to the law of sin which is in my members. O wretched man that I am! Who shall deliver me from the body of this death? I Thank God through Jesus Christ our Lord. So then with the mind I myself serve the law of God; but with the flesh the law of sin"* ~Romans 7:25

The Encounter had brought me face to face with some of the things that I should have done differently as a Christian and I had come to terms with the fact that I had made the mistake of trying to fight a spiritual battle with natural weapons. I was always calm on the outside even when I was very angry on the inside. I refused to continue to blame my ex-manager because I began to realize that she did what she had always done. For me to expect something different of her was foolishness on my part. I was the only person that I had the ability to change in the situation. Her lies had angered me, I found her actions unprofessional but I was working under a different code of ethics and my expectations were unreasonable. It was pride that made me think that I could change the situation. I decided to accept the responsibility for everything and to forgive her because

I knew that no matter how hard I worked on my vision, it would go nowhere without true forgiveness.

I will never forget the day that I was driving on I20 in Atlanta when I thought that I saw the woman who I worked with at the bank who had acted as a buffer between me and my ex-manager driving by in another car, I had an intense urge to run the car off of the road. Thank God I resisted the urge. That was when I realized that I still had some un-forgiveness. When I left the office on my final day, I had hugged everyone including my manager but months had passed and my life had begun to really suffer because of the job loss, I kept as much as I could from my family because I didn't want them to worry. Our savings were all gone and the house was in foreclosure. I knew that I could forgive in a time of plenty but could I forgive in a time of lack? I learned that I could.

After this reflection and introspection, I adopted a posture of humility, biblical humility, not what the average person calls humility, there is a difference. Biblical humility releases all preconceived ideas and submits to the Word and the will of God. The world's definition of humility is to allow you to be mistreated and downtrodden but the biblical view is to allow God to handle everything and not to be concerned about anything. That type of humility requires a higher level of trust in God but it does not mean to be mistreated and downtrodden. My understanding of humility and trust before were skewed because of training and life events that prevented me from seeing things according to the Kingdom. I saw the attack through the eyes of generational injustice and prejudice and not through the eyes of someone who Jesus Christ had set free. Even all the years of excellent biblical teaching had not penetrated the walls in my soul (mind, will and emotions) to a point where I was able to walk in true biblical humility and love.

Adversity will do either one of two things make you bitter or make you better, you choose. When going through adversity you are either going to believe the enemy's lies or the truth of God's Word but the responsibility to course correct your actions and beliefs are yours not God's. Not all adversity is because you did something wrong, sometimes it comes because you've done something right. Sometimes generational un-forgiveness and hurt (perpetual un-forgiveness that has continued from generation to generation) as well as our own disappointing life experiences can sabotage our efforts to be Christ like. Wherever there is an effect, there is a cause.

> "As the bird by wandering, as the swallow by flying, so the curse causeless shall not come" ~Proverbs 26: 2

I thought that I could get God to follow my plan rather than submitting to His plan but I was wrong. The time that I spent reflecting showed me that my core values were strong. I had been taught as a child to respect those in authority but I had also been taught not to allow anyone to disrespect me.

God didn't have a problem with me being proud of my ancestors or the accomplishments that He had helped me to make, the pride that God hated was the pride that told me that I could change the situation using my own methods. It was my lack of trust in Him that saddened Him. His concerns were about my character. The adversity brought on by my pride, fear and unfinished emotional baggage, positioned me in a place to be shaped in the hands of God and receptive to His use.

I had to come to a place of complete surrender to reflect on where God had brought me from and what He had taken me through and to remember who I was in Him. I knew that the enemy was after my confidence, my determination and my true testimony but I also knew that before this loss, I had become so comfortable that I never shared my real testimony. I seldom thought about how far I had come.

Now, more than ever, I was determined not to give into this temporary defeat but rather I was more determined than ever to see exactly what God had in mind. Pride and fear had played major roles but now they had been replaced by love, faith and submission.

> *"The question is not" Are you going to fail?" The question is "How are you going to handle your failure?"* ~John C. Maxwell

The training that I received as a child, an adolescent, and young adult, the street smarts that I learned in New York in the early years, the upward movement through the ranks of Corporate America (including the job loss) had all made a deposit and contributed to me being me. I began to see that when I thought that I had arrived, I had not arrived at all, I had just ended another phase of training. The years in the hair salon and the years in Corporate America were only training. I had become so comfortable in my profession that if things had not happened exactly as they had, I would have never gone to the next level. Are there other ways to go to the next level? Yes, I'm sure there are but for me this time, this was my experience.

I traced the line of events that had led me up to this point and I knew that my destiny was unfolding before me. If I had not accepted the transfer to Atlanta from New York, I would probably still be working in Corporate Trust on Wall Street but I would not be writing, speaking and coaching. I would not be a licensed minister or have experienced the many things that I have experienced.

My grandparents instilled a strength in me that caused me to be tenacious and resilient, I knew that everything would work out as long as I kept my focus on Jesus Christ;

He is the author and finisher of my faith. Who am I? I am tough perhaps shaped by too many hard times; I am a worshipper who yields to the presence of the Holy Spirit. I am a mother, a sister, an aunt, a grandmother, a daughter, and a friend, and although the enemy wanted to use this ordeal to destroy me, I knew that God had used it to make me better. With a change of my focus I began to write, I knew that God would keep me during the turbulent times ahead. God's methods may change but His ways never do. He is always faithful.

> *"Blessing I will bless you, and multiplying I will multiply your descendants as the stars of the heaven and as the sand which is on the seashore; and your descendants shall possess the gate of their enemies" ~Genesis 22:17*

First I looked to God because I needed to know that my relationship with Him was intact. Secondly, I took a long reflective look at my life because I needed to remember my past and reflect upon how far God had brought me. Thirdly, I took a look inside of myself because I needed to remember who I was in the natural as well as in Him because my uniqueness is rooted in both places. This approach helped me to prepare for the future and it will continue to serve me as I walk into my destiny; God first, my testimony (what and how God has brought me through), and who I am in Him (what I learned through the Word and by my experiences).

The word that God had given me was beginning to take shape but more slowly than I wanted it to. I was still unemployed and although I had searched diligently for a job for months, I still didn't have one. Each interview seemed to go well but then I would not get the job. I was tempted to leave Georgia several times because there were other Corporate Trust positions available elsewhere but I knew that leaving Georgia would be a mistake. I still believed that Georgia was where I was supposed to be, I could have gone back to New York but instead I decided to stand in faith and see what God would do. After all, it wouldn't take any faith to pull up stakes and go home but to stay in Georgia took every ounce of faith that I had.

I worked on a few temporary jobs and then a lady that attended my church asked if I would consider taking a three month temporary assignment as a secretary where she worked. She knew that I had been a vice president but what she didn't know was that at that time, I would have considered taking any job! One of her co-workers was going on maternity leave soon and they were looking for someone to replace the secretary who happened to be replacing the woman going on maternity leave.

I quickly said yes although I had no secretarial skills to speak of and she arranged for the interview. The day of the interview, I walked out of my house to find that my car had a flat tire (I had never had a flat tire before). I had arranged to follow my friend's car as she drove to work, since I didn't know how to get to the interview. Having a flat tire meant that I could not follow her; it also meant that I would be late for the interview. I phoned my friend who was waiting for me in the nearby Kroger parking lot and told her that I had a flat tire. She went to work and informed them about the situation. I phoned my car insurance company who came out and changed the tire. I finally made it to the interview later that day.

I interviewed for the position and was given the job the same day. My Christian sister didn't know it but at that time I had one mortgage payment left in my bank account, all of my savings were gone. The hand of God was evident. God gave me such favor that the three month contract lasted for years and included several job title changes and pay increases. As they say "when God closes a door He opens a window." God proved to me that He was my source and that His grace was sufficient for me. The position wasn't glamorous and some would say that it was a step backwards but I knew that it was a conduit for provision. Because it was a contract position, it was also a faith builder.

The way the position became available was clearly a display of God's grace. After months of unemployment and one mortgage payment away from being totally out of money, I got a job. In the natural it was uncomfortable for me because in my mind, it was a contract position, it had no stability. I was walking on the water! The position paid much less than I earned at the bank but I knew that God was working everything out.

My first position at this job was to work in the secretarial position while the secretary filled the more technical position left empty by the woman on maternity leave. The day that I had the interview, I sat with the secretary for a few moments to go over her duties. I was told to come in the next day for the secretary to continue to train me to work in her position for the next few months but when I reported to work, the secretary was not there. She phoned in later that day and quit which made her position open and available. My first week in the new position my car was rear ended, hit from behind by a speeding car. I lost the use of my car until the repairs were completed but because I still had the car insurance that I had while I worked at the bank, I was able to have a car rental at no cost until my car was repaired. Thank you Jesus!

After a month in that position, I was moved into another position, one with more responsibility and a higher rate of pay. In this position, I was able to use some of the skills that I had acquired over the years in my former profession; I still was not earning as much as I had at the bank but God was showing me something new about money and finance, how to survive when there wasn't enough. When I changed positions, I had the opportunity to recommend a friend for the secretarial position and she was hired. Not only did God bless me, He allowed me to be a blessing to my friend. I knew that God was working everything out but He wasn't doing it according to my understanding or my timing.

I was still slowly moving in the direction that the Lord was leading me in but I was very careful because I did not want to get ahead of Him. I felt like I was being held in a holding pattern like an airplane that is scheduled to land at a busy airport. I was instructed to circle until I was given instructions by the tower to land. I could not begin to descend until cleared for landing. It was not time for me to land but it was time for me to circle, I was definitely in a holding pattern and I knew that as long as I had enough fuel, I would be alright. I also knew that it was important for me to listen to the tower because when the instruction was given, I could not hesitate to move. Although I could not move as quickly toward the dream as I would have liked, I was content knowing that in God's timing everything would be made perfect.

Although for me it was important to take a look inside some people have simply put their past under the blood of Jesus and moved on without delving deeply in their past and that worked for them. That was the approach that I had taken before when I transitioned into Corporate America. I turned my back on my past and moved into my future full speed ahead and for years God was so faithful that I had not thought about my past in years. It took the adversity to break away all of the buried areas and walls and to replace them with true faith.

Introspection can be good for a limited amount of time but too much introspection can become procrastination and keep you from moving into the future. I began to understand that my faith, my attitude and everything that was in me had been challenged at a very high level. I knew that my life and my future were in God's hands and when I cooperated with Him no dream that I might have would be too large.

Fighting the Good Fight of Faith

Ironic as it may sound; when I was fighting to clear myself on the job (which I thought was faith) every explanation that I provided was cast aside and deemed an excuse. I really didn't begin to walk in true faith until I had nothing; God got all of my attention. It's unfortunate but it is common among Christians to come to know what faith is when their back is against the wall and they have no ability to change their own circumstances. Building faith requires trust. Trust is difficult to achieve for people who have been damaged by some of life's circumstances but with God all things are possible. Fighting the good fight of faith requires that you relinquish your rights to fight using carnal means. There are times when God will instruct you to do something that makes no sense in the natural but when the instruction is acted upon, it has amazing breakthrough results.

In I Timothy 6: 12, Paul admonished Timothy to fight the good fight of faith because Paul knew that it is a fight that has to be fought for Timothy to achieve everything related to his confession and call. To hold onto your faith is a fight that must be fought with deliberate perseverance, following after righteousness, godliness, faith, love, patience and meekness.

I had to be willing to fight the good fight of faith regardless of the circumstances; the circumstances included my successes and my failures. No matter what the circumstance, God had a plan for my life and His plan required that I knew how to fight the good fight of faith because for a believer knowing how to fight the good fight of faith is required.

Part II

CHAPTER 4

The Process Can Be Painful

From the time that I reached Georgia I was impressed by its beauty. My life situation was perfect. I retained my New York job and salary and the bank paid all of the relocation expense. After two years, I purchased a home and then after a bizarre head on collision that totaled my car, I leased a new car.

After a year of visiting churches, I finally found the church in Georgia that I believe God had directed me to and I joined the church. This church was perfect. With the exception of my work situation, my life in Georgia was like a dream, everything was wonderful.

> *"Search me, O God, and know my heart: try me and know my thoughts; and see if there be any wicked way in me, and lead me in the way everlasting"~ Psalm 141:23-247*

When God provided for me to move to Georgia, I didn't know what I would find in Georgia but I went anyway because I recognized God's leading. Now, I realize several things; God knew exactly what would be there and He did not give me all of the information. God knew better than I what I was capable of handling. After the job loss, I still believed that God intended for me to stay in Georgia; I had to make some decisions. Would I stay or would I go, would I sell the house and move into an apartment or keep the house, would I continue to believe God when things became uncomfortable or would I take things into my own hands? The temptation to leave Georgia came every time I tried to find a job that was comparable to my last position. The temptation to leave arrived each month when the bills came and I saw my savings account and then my 401K get smaller and smaller. At one point, I said to myself, "when this account gets to ten thousand dollars, I'm out of here," but when it did I still didn't have a release in my spirit to leave.

Some of the decisions that I made during this time were very uncomfortable for me, although the decisions went against my logical and analytical mind, I decided not to leave Georgia; I decided not to sell the house. I decided to take the road less traveled and to totally depend on God. I knew that what had happened to me was a destiny event and that what I did next would affect me for the rest of my life. I tried to come to terms with the past as I began to plan for my future.

> *"Great things are not done by impulse but by a series of small things brought together"* ~Unknown

Before this, I thought that I knew what it meant to "walk by faith," but my decision to stay in Georgia, because I believed God wanted me to stay there added a totally new dimension to that term "faith." The walk required all of the courage and determination that I had. I had gone through testing and trials before but never like this. The test of the past seemed more like an annoyance like a fly buzzing around your head. Although, I'm sure that during those times of test and trials, they seemed just as difficult, but they could not compare to this. Each day I was faced with something else, another problem. Usually the problems were financial but sometimes they were emotional or spiritual and some days they were all of these at the same time.

I love a good metaphor or analogy and I think that Bishop T.D. Jakes has an excellent way of telling a story. It was very timely that during this period he decided to teach on "Potholes on the Road to Destiny." Being from the north, I fully understood the analogy. In the north because of the amount of snowfall the transportation or sanitation departments spread a salt mixture on the roads and the mixture melts the snow and ice. The problem is that although the salt mixture melts the snow and ice it also destroys the roads. The salt and chemicals produce large holes in the roads, these holes are called potholes. Some of the potholes are small but others are large enough to swallow the front end of an automobile and can cause substantial damage to a vehicle.

Using Bishops Jake's analogy, I knew that I had hit a major pothole and that it would take a period of time to recover. I had to deal with it in every area of my life; spiritual, physical, social and financial. First; I dealt with it physically by getting some much needed rest. Secondly, I became more actively involved in my church, I had more free time and I used it by volunteering and serving more. I attended classes at church and graduated from several classes there. Spiritually, I reviewed my part in what happened and accepted my responsibility in the situation, repented and acknowledged that God was not finished with me yet! Financially, I used my savings and liquidated some assets as I continued to look for another job in Georgia.

> "Thine eyes did see my substance, yet being unperfect; and in thy book all my members were written, which in continuance were fashioned, when as yet there was none of them" ~Psalm 141:16

During the time, while still working out the "pothole" issues, especially in the area of finance because when I did finally get a job, my income dropped 33 percent but my expenses remained the same. I tried multilevel marketing but I didn't have much success. I continued to look for a full time permanent position but no doors opened and I admit that I eventually stopped looking. There was no doubt that I had been given favor on the contract job but because it was a contract job it could end at any time and that made me uncomfortable. It required faith and total trust in God; I tried to look for the good in every situation.

I believed that I would find a job soon and I continued to remain thankful to God for the contract position that He had provided. Eventually, I realized that I was there for a reason and when it was time to move, God would let me know. It wasn't until I submitted to that discovery that I began to experience some peace about my job situation, which allowed me to focus and work more attentively on my vision.

Every day was a walk in and by faith. Since God had provided my present position so miraculously, I knew that when the time came, He could do it again. Each time that my contract ended it was extended or renewed with a pay increase. For the first time since I arrived in Georgia most of the people I worked with were genuinely friendly I didn't have to think about hidden agendas. Eventually I stopped beating myself up about what had happened at the bank and realized that even with my own contribution, most of what went on was due to other people's insecurities. Even with the favor and pay increases in the contract position, I knew that without a miracle from God, this position would never become permanent, it was that type of position. I believe in miracles but I was also aware that this job and the day to day uncertainty of it had significance; it helped me to keep my trust in God.

One day I received one of those emails that circulate in offices, it contained a series of questions which were asked of a silversmith, and I found his answers interesting. The questions that were asked were related to the refining of silver, here are his answers in summary:

> The silversmith holds the piece of silver over the flame to let it heat up; he has to hold it in the middle of the flame where the flames are the hottest as to burn away any impurities.

> The silversmith has to sit there the entire time with the silver, watching it closely, because if it is left in the flame a moment too long it will be destroyed.

> The silversmith will know when the silver is fully refined because he can see his image in it.

The story rang in my heart because I recognized the silversmith as God and me as the silver. God was with me He never left me but he saw what needed to be removed and the process required fire. It required flames so hot that every impurity was burned away. But even when the flames were at their hottest God would not remove me until what needed to be accomplished was completed and He could see His reflection in me. I had to trust Him.

> "He will sit as a refiner and a purifier of silver; He will purify the sons of Levi, and purge them as gold and silver, that they may offer to the Lord An offering in righteousness"~ Malachi 3:3

I decided to stop wasting time on a job search and to begin to place my focus in the direction where I believed that the Lord was leading me. I began to prepare for a call that I knew absolutely nothing about. It was a challenge for me because I like very detailed instructions and there weren't any. I started by using the skills, talents and abilities that I already had. I knew that In order for me to change the things in my life that needed to be changed, I had to begin to think differently and to learn some new skills. That meant that I had to be flexible and teachable. God was molding me and shaping me into another vessel and at times it was very painful.

Although there were many problems the resolution of each problem built in me endurance and resilience and moved me closer to my goal. With each financial challenge there was a plan and an execution of that plan to get me out of that particular situation. Some of those plans worked and some didn't. Solving some of the problems reminded me of the things that I liked about Corporate Trust ; I liked working on the accounts that were not what we called "cookie Cutters" or "black and white," there was a degree of difficulty in them; I liked dealing with the more complicated and complex bond financings.

Working through the problems also showed me that I had been more diligent in the management of the Corporate Trust accounts than I had been in my own personal accounts. Although at the beginning of the crisis, I had a financial cushion now I wished that I had saved more. I never planned for being without work for a long period of time.

Apart from my investments, I realized that my philosophy about money had not changed much from before I started working in Corporate Trust. I had diligently worked on and improved in my professional career and I had become an expert at handling bond trust funds but that knowledge had only transferred moderately in my own personal finances. I should have been far more diligent with my own money.

Now I was at a place in my life where my thinking about money had to change. I was raised and trained to be an employee and I believed that because I was a good employee, I would always have a job but the world has changed. Throughout this crisis every time God revealed something to me it was to teach me or to bring my attention to an area that He intended to use. I was moving into two years since my job loss and even with the bills and the expenses, we were still in the house. Hallelujah!

More Problems

The volume and weight of the problems were a real challenge because it seemed that things happened all at once. The timing of each problem was very close to another, as soon as one was solved another showed up. I had to prioritize everything and decide which problem to solve first. I knew that something had to change. I explored several options; downsizing into an apartment with four other people in tow did not appeal to me, job searches outside of Georgia where I could work and send money home and commute on the weekends definitely was not the answer. Although I did seriously consider a Corporate Trust job offer in Alabama! When I decided to sell the house, the quotes that I received were unacceptable. Finally, under pressure, I decided that if another opportunity for employment opened outside of Georgia, I would take it, but no doors opened

> "And beside this, giving all diligence, add to your faith virtue; and to virtue knowledge; and to knowledge temperance; and to temperance patience; and to patience godliness; and to godliness brotherly kindness; and to brotherly kindness charity. For if these things be in you, and abound, they make you that ye shall neither be barren nor unfruitful in the knowledge of our Lord Jesus Christ" ~2 Peter 1: 5-8

I fasted often and prayed continually, my flesh was extremely uncomfortable in the beginning and then after a period of time I began to rest in faith. The rest of faith is that place in the Spirit unlike any other, nothing bothers you. You understand in a way that supersedes your mind and mental abilities that God has you. You know how to cast your cares on the Lord. You sleep like a baby when the threat of foreclosure looms about you. By the time you reach the rest of faith, you have faced more obstacles then you thought that you would be able to face even with God's help. What once seemed impossible becomes possible.

I learned to be thankful at times when I had not gotten what I had prayed for. And when I looked at the household spending at the end of each year, it did not make any sense by God's grace we had come through another year. I learned to surrender more fully to God and to allow my decisions to be founded on my trust in Him, because I knew that I could not come up with a scenario that would work. I learned trust, dependence and faith on an entirely different level. I'm sure that there are those who will say "there is no way that she could have been in the Will of God," I'm sorry, you're wrong; I have never been as much in the Will of God as I was during this period of my life.

Sometimes we are so busy trying to determine if it is God or the devil causing our circumstances, we don't examine the purpose behind the circumstances, or our contributions to the circumstances, we try to use a formula when what we need is to know the mind of God. It is when we reach an impasse, that we understand scriptures like "Be still and know that I am God." Is that faith? Yes, I believe that it is. I can tell you from experience that without faith, I could not have continued to stand. I could have easily changed my situation by leaving Georgia and had a good salary in New York working in Corporate Trust but that would have taken no faith at all. It took faith for me to stay where I believed that God wanted for me to be.

My desire was to see what God would do with my obedience. God was not punishing me, God was providing for me in a difficult situation. There were many reasons why things were the way that they were but my decision was to complete this situation trusting in God to get me through every decision and the attack of the enemy.

> "But without faith it is impossible o please Him: for he that cometh to God must believe that He is, and that He is a rewarder of them that diligently seek Him" ~Hebrews 11:6

My understanding of statements in scripture like; be strong in the Lord, dwell in the secret place of the Most High, having done all to stand, stand therefore, and others, made more sense to me now, they were my reality. The scriptures that I once memorized to quote suddenly had new meaning and leaped off of the page and became real. They were all that I had and through them I saw God's work on a daily basis. My spirit developed, my flesh was controlled and my mind had to surrender to the leadership of my spirit as I yielded to the Holy Spirit

The Building Process

When construction is being done on a new building, the depth of the excavation for the foundation depends on how tall the finished building will be. The height of the building determines how deeply the foundation will be dug. The foundation must be able to support the building. The best materials are used when building a skyscraper. The best architect is used to draft the plans. Sometimes a lot of destruction may have to take place before the construction can begin, especially if something else once stood where the new building is being erected. Whatever was on the site before has to be demolished and the debris has to be taken away. When the ground is clear, additional heavy equipment is brought in to break up the ground and to start digging for the new foundation. The entire time, trucks are carting away debris.

Now, I'm not a building but I know when I'm under construction. I could tell by the heavy equipment that the enemy had used, that his intention was to destroy me. But, if Satan's plan was for my destruction, God's plan was for my construction. My responsibility was to stand and learn all that I could while going through the trials, distractions and obstacles that accompanied the process. The things that we call success many times are not success to God, but merely stepping stones along the way. Success to God is when His goal and His purpose have been reached. His vision is much broader than our vision. His plans and purposes are higher than our plans and purposes.

> *"As for God, His way is perfect: the word of the Lord is tried: He is a buckler to all those that trust Him" ~Psalm 18:30*

Unlike the building of a skyscraper as described above where everything has a specific phase, going through the process that I was going through was strange because demolition and construction were going on simultaneously. There was no neat formula to follow. I had to be sensitive to recognize when something was being taken out of my life to be replaced with something else. I learned to not always attribute loss to Satan; sometimes it is God who is removing something from your life because it is not what He wants for you. At other times the enemy is trying to give you something that you have to recognize and refuse, regardless of how good it may seem.

My attitude toward things changed in an awesome way. I changed in a way that only God could have accomplished the changes in such a short amount of time. I began to understand the power of humility, things were out of my control; I developed a trust and dependence on God as He took on the challenges on my behalf. It occurred to me that this is what He meant before my job loss when He told me to fight, but I didn't realize He meant to surrender to Him and to humble myself and I did not understand.

My years as a single parent and the years spent in Corporate America had given me a "taking on the world" mentality and that mentality had gotten in God's way. I was so use to "making it happen" that in order for me to be still and know that He was God, I had to come to a point of realization that my decisions were only good when they were based on my understanding of God's strength, power and His ways. Not everyone has to go through this type of process but I did, it was necessary for me.

Changing My Mind

I had a fresh prospective on everything. My focus changed to my calling, purpose and future. Since I was doing everything that I knew to do, I realized that I had come to a place in my life where I had never been before and I knew that it would take a new mindset to achieve what God wanted. I started to re-read some of the books in my library with a different motivation. I have a habit of re-reading books so I usually purchase what I read rather than to borrow from the library, I like to highlight and underline sections that provide me with new or relevant information that has specific interest to me at that time. I had to renew my mind about what was going on in my life currently as well as for what I saw in my future.

I was tempted at first to attribute everything that had happened to me as something that was God sent rather than God used. Even my theology, what I believed about God was challenged. After years of being in church and being taught by excellent bible teachers some of the early childhood teachings were still in my mind. Rather than to replace the old with the new, the new was sitting on top of the old and that came to the surface when my belief system was challenged. I had to choose the doctrine to follow. There are many doctrines and theologies in the body of Christ, I had to choose the one that I believed was true and decide to stand by it and not to be moved."

I realized that I had an employee mentality and that my getting another job would not bring me any closer to my purpose and what God had in mind for me. I needed to learn more about being an entrepreneur, having a small business or ministry. These things were all related to my purpose.

I got a vision for a company and I started building the infrastructure of the company. I began to write my first book, and the writing came naturally, it didn't take long for me to complete the book. Each time that I had an idea and moved forward, doors opened toward the realization of the idea. There was no doubt in my mind or in my heart that I was on the right path.

> *"If at first you do succeed do something harder"* ~John C. Maxwell

Trying to understand exactly where I was in the big scheme of things, seeing the big picture was difficult, at the same time that I was going through a difficult time, I was experiencing a wonderful time of adventure. While I was struggling in one area of my life the Lord was blessing me in another area of my life, it was a strange experience. I organized and incorporated the company, wrote and published my first book and continued to organize and work on the vision of the company.

Even then I continued to miss Corporate Trust, it was a large part of my life for a long time and I still felt the loss.

CHAPTER 5

Coming to Terms

I can describe the year that I left the bank in the same terms that Charles Dickens describes in the opening lines of A Tell of Two Cities, "It was the best of times; it was the worst of times." I was at the height of my career but I had a manager who was anxious for my departure. For entirely too long I had tried to work in a situation that eventually ended with my forced resignation. Now, it was time to put closure to the issue of my job loss. The time of rehearsing over and over again what could have been done differently had to end. I needed to use that energy toward my future.

There was one other thing that I needed to do in order for that to happen, I needed to remember the facts as they really were. Over time, I had examined my contribution so closely that I no longer thought about how others had contributed to the situation. The enemy had played back my contributions to the situation in my mind so many times that I had almost forgotten what things were done to me. I went through a lot of "should have, could have, would have," before I finally realized that none of that really mattered. The truth was that I had come to a place in my life the only way that I could have. Every obstacle, every roadblock, every twist and turn was meant to carry me to the next level in my life. Without the challenges to my faith, my faith would be weak and unsustainable at the next level.

When I came to terms with all that had occurred, I could say that I had remained true to my convictions, regardless of the current circumstances, I could still look at myself in the mirror and know that everything was going to be alright. It took courage to take the stand that I took and courage was one of the things that I would need to take me into my future. It reminded me of the story that I once heard about a butterfly who was struggling to get out of its cocoon when someone who thought that they were helping it freed it from its cocoon thereby eliminating its struggle. Because the butterfly was freed prematurely without the struggle needed to fully develop its wings, it was never able to fly. While I hated the struggle, I knew that I needed the struggle.

God always works according to a pattern based on a principal. God had faithfully given me a word knowing that I would need it to sustain me through one of the most difficult times of my life. He only said two words and from those two words everything began to emerge. I submitted everything to God because I knew that He would only honor my plans if they agreed with His plans. I determined to prepare for where I believed He was taking me. I knew that all I needed to do was to rely on the guidance of the Holy Spirit. I had to trust Him and believe that His plan was the best thing for me.

I had already undergone enough to know to stay in God's Will. I continued to work on the infrastructure of the company and to write. I developed a sense of appreciation for the business and started a quarterly e-newsletter which soon became a monthly e-newsletter; it immediately began to impact people's lives. We developed a monthly feature to showcase entrepreneurs and ministers.

These individuals had stepped out in faith toward their God given destiny so we featured them in our e-newsletter and on our website to give them more exposure and to encourage them. I began to notice that when I was working on the vision, I had a sense of satisfaction that made up for the hard work and sacrifice. Our e-newsletter subscriber list began to grow and the hits to our web site increased. We began to receive e-mails from around the world which really surprised me and then letters; we started a radio broadcast on Blog Talk Radio and developed an on-line presence on multiple social Media sites. I began speaking and produced a CD and DVD. The vision finally began to take shape.

> *"As Life's battles don't always go to the stronger or faster man. But sooner or later the man who wins is the man who thinks he can"*
> ~Unknown

Doors began to open as we followed the plan. Initially, the plans were very limited because of several factors but I realized that God was in control and was directing my steps. I had to become sensitive enough to the Holy Spirit to know when to move forward and when to stay still, when to act swiftly and when to pace my actions slowly. I learned the difference between time and timing. I also knew better than to get in front of God, I determined to always follow His lead. Something else was happening in me; I was getting excited about what I was doing. I stopped worrying about financial difficulties and decided to take one day at a time. I decided to move forward with the vision.

There are times when the company, In His Season, Inc. or I have helped someone else with their vision, or when someone tells me about how much the book or the e-newsletter has helped or encouraged them and that encourages me and helps me to see God's plan unfolding.

Whenever for some reason I would get discouraged God would always send a word, a person or reminder to encourage me and give some indication that I was on the right course. I saw God take the few dollars that we had for promotion of the business and finance promotions. He continues to show me over and over again through His faithfulness that I was on the right course. Thinking about it now, losing my job may have been the best thing that could have happened to me at that time. I decided to use former successes as stepping stones and I used my former mistakes as lessons to grow from. I began to get a glimpse at what God saw in me and I moved toward it.

> *"Now the just shall live by faith: but if any man draw back, my soul shall have no pleasure in him. But we are not of them who draw back unto perdition; but of them that believe to the saving of the soul" ~Hebrews 10:38-39*

The Turning Point

I still had a love for Corporate Trust and from time to time usually when I didn't have any money, I would go online to the Monster.com website and look at all of the Corporate Trust positions that were available, it was like self-torture. I think that I continued to look to prove something to myself, that Corporate Trust was still an option if things became too difficult. Each time I decided not to pursue any of the positions. I always consoled myself by saying "I'm a Certified Corporate Trust Specialist

(CCTS), I earned it and no one can take that from me" somehow that always made me feel better.

I was having a great time with the vision that God had given me but I continued looking back from time to time. Even though most of my focus was on the vision there was still a part of me that longed for the Corporate Trust world. I missed the bond closings and the account management, meetings with clients, traveling to network meetings and discussing deals. I missed the business.

For seventeen years I had moved steadily up through the ranks of Corporate Trust. I had sacrificed time with my children to attend college so that we could have a better life and now it seemed that everything associated with that part of my life was gone. In my mind the only thing that I had left to prove that seventeen years of my life counted for anything was my CCTS. As long as I could maintain the continuing education credits and pay the annual membership fee, I could maintain the certification. I remember that I was the first person in my office in New York to receive the coveted "CCTS" designation showing that I was a specialist in the field of Corporate Trust, everyone in the office was proud of me.

Our most senior managers in the office were all from Morgan Guaranty Trust Company, a very elite group of professionals. Even they applauded my determination and achievement. I hadn't gone the regular route but had done some intensive self-study which along with my years in the business and a recommendation from a senior person in the industry was sufficient for me to take the exam. It was an honor to be a Certified Corporate Trust Specialist.

I remembered an occasion when one of our sales professionals was confronted by a senior manager and replied "yes, you are a CCTS but you were grandfathered in, Teresita actually took the test, she earned it." I was surprised that he would insert me into their conversation but I understood what he meant. When the industry began offering the CCTS designation, anyone who had been in the industry for a certain number of years could receive the designation without taking the test, they were "grandfathered" in and given the designation if they applied for it.

The CCTS designation was something that I had earned and I wanted to keep it but eventually even that became something that had to go.

One year I attended a meeting in Alabama for Corporate Trust Professionals. I attended the meeting because I needed to earn continuing education credit hours to maintain my CCTS certification. I saw a few people there I knew from the bank including my ex-manager's ex-manager, he served on the Diversity Counsel in Charlotte with me but He had left the bank shortly before I did. I also saw some people from the first bank that I worked at in Georgia and they were no longer at that bank.

I felt no bitterness toward any of them, I greeted all of them with a smile, a hand shake or a hug; it was good to see them. I had taken two vacation days off of work to attend this two day Corporate Trust Meeting. I had also passed up a potential speaking engagement to attend this meeting.

> "The successful man will profit from his mistakes and try again in a different way" ~Dale Carnegie

On the drive to the meeting, a still small voice inside of me asked "what are you doing" and I ignored it and I continued to make the two and a half hour drive to the meeting. In my mind and my heart, no matter what anyone had done to me or what I had been through, the truth was that I was still a Certified Corporate Trust Specialist and no one could take that away from me. I was determined to keep my certification, and I ignored the small voice inside me and continued to make my way to the meeting.

When I arrived at the meeting place I took a seat and began to listen to the various speakers and presenters. There were presentations about computer systems, regulatory updates, and new case law. But the presentation that impacted me the most I still remember. What I remember is that it had very little to do with technical

Corporate Trust issues this presentation was titled "The Purple Cow" and it was about innovation. It was nothing like the other presentations, while I sat there and listened to the various speakers, rather than being interested in the information that was being presented on Corporate Trust, I was critiquing their presentation skill and the flow of their presentations because that was what I had been doing since I left Corporate Trust. The technical information was the same old stuff and wasn't interesting at all.

Once again, that still small voice said "what are you doing here?' After the speaker completed the Purple Cow presentation, we got into groups for a breakout session our instructions were to come up with a creative idea.

> *"I have often thought that the best way to define a man's character would be to seek out the particular mental or moral attitude in which, when it came upon him, he felt himself most deeply and intensely active and alive"*
> *~William James*

I was ready; I was excited to come up with a creative idea after the Purple Cow presentation. I had been coming up with creative ideas for the past two years. When I got into my group the group leader already had an idea so all I needed to do was to contribute to the idea by making suggestions. I jumped right in with my suggestions, it was great! But as I looked around the circle where we were gathered, I saw that the others in the circle were silent. Their posture was very rigid; it was easy to see that they were uncomfortable. Before we began the presenter said that everyone was required to participate, and that if anyone didn't participate they would be expelled from the group (humor intended to cause everyone to participate) but no one in my group said anything. They seemed reluctant to participate.

As I sat there making my contributions to the creative exercise, I thought about the Purple Cow presentation and the comments of the presenter and I thought, he is right and I realized that I was probably the only one in the room who understood what he was really talking about. He was talking about change, drastic out of the box change; I knew what that was like. He was asking them to make the changes that he thought was necessary to prevent their industry from dying, but the faces in the room didn't appear to reflect any interest in change. Tradition was the order of the day. As we returned to our regular seats again from the circle of chairs that we had formed for the breakout session, the still small voice on the inside of me repeated again "what are you doing here" this time I answered "I don't know."

"If something has been done a particular way for fifteen or twenty years, it's a pretty good sign, in these changing times, that it is being done the wrong way" ~Elliot M. Estes

We got a ten minute brake and I went outside to phone one of my friends. This was a friend who I'd know for a long time, we worked together in Corporate Trust in New York. I told her "I am not feeling this at all" she knew where I was and why I was there, as we spoke; I realized that this was a destiny moment. A destiny moment is a point in time that defines who you are and sets you on a path or in a certain direction. I was about to leave my past and enter into my future. The love that I once had for Corporate Trust was over; I had no desire to stay until the end of the session or to return for the sessions the next day. It was over. I just wanted to leave there so I did.

It didn't make any sense for me to maintain the certification, for what? What was I trying to prove? Who was I trying to impress? I had been there, done that, and no one could deny that, I needed to move on. I wanted to kick myself for passing up an opportunity to speak at a women's event to attend this Corporate Trust event. I began to realize that as long as I kept looking back, the focus that I needed to walk into my future would be divided. With no hesitation, I picked up my portfolio and headed to my car for the long drive home.

I had finally come to the revelation that my career in Corporate Trust was over. The presentation about the "Purple Cow" and the comments by the speaker had awakened two things in me: I knew that I no longer needed the CCTS, every dollar and every moment of time that I used toward keeping it was time and money taken away from my vision. There were certifications, training and other expenses related to my future. I had a decision to make, do I hold onto my past or let it go completely to embrace a future that I was still uncertain of at times. The other revelation was that I could continue to use the designation because, people outside of the industry didn't recognize its significance anyway so, if I referred to the certification as "former" or "current" it had the same relevance! I decided to let it go.

CHAPTER 6

Embracing the Change

Transition is defined as the process or a period of changing from one state or condition to another. Transitions can be difficult, going from the familiar to the unfamiliar just does not agree with human nature. When the transition is intentional and planned like when I moved from Washington D. C. to New York, there is anticipation for the new: new relationships, new places, new adventures and new learning experiences. My move from New York, NY to Atlanta, GA had also been exciting but also difficult because I left friends behind.

I knew that when making a transition I needed to be prepared to expect the unexpected. But this transition from my old life to my new life was far more difficult than I thought it would be. This transition out of Corporate Trust was thrust upon me and it came at a time when by all of my expectations, I was set for life; I was comfortable physically, financially and spiritually. For the first time since I had decided to change my life years before by attending college, getting g off of welfare and changing careers, I reached the place in life that I wanted to be. But now, I was starting over in a completely new direction at the age of fifty. One minute I was riding high in my career and the next minute I was without a job. The swiftness and severity left me in a mental fog at first but I understood that this event was really more of a shift in direction than anything else.

In my Corporate Trust career I had become accustomed to rapid change. Things were constantly in flux, legislative changes, computer system changes, procedural changes, banks merging, all of these things affected the business. From the onset of the era of mergers and acquisition when many banks sold off their Corporate Trust business to other banks things could change very quickly so change was common place.

I realized early in my career that in order to remain competitive in my field, I had to adapt to change quickly. I aggressively pursued change when it was related to my career. But I must admit that in my personal life, I did not have the same philosophy. I liked the comfort of sameness. Like most people, I did things occasionally to break up the monotony like an occasional vacation and some form of entertainment but I lived safely within my comfort zone. The loss of my job forced me into a new paradigm. It forced me to take a good look at my choices and priorities. When I took a serious look I found that I was unprepared to experience the loss of everything that I had worked so hard to obtain. I felt unprepared to pursue what God had set before me, I was in transition.

Being a Christian and living the life of a Christian made the loss initially seem more difficult. As the saying goes "I don't drink, smoke, or chew or hang around with people who do!' I was saved, sanctified and filled with the Holy Spirit. I served in the church and paid my tithes and offerings but it wasn't until I got off of the rollercoaster that I called my professional life that I was able to see clearly. For me to think that I was exempt from being hurt, offended, lied on rejected wasn't realistic or biblical.

Often I read the bible putting myself in the shoes of the characters only after they have become victorious. I seldom examined the difficulties, the internal and external struggles that the characters confronted before they achieved the victory. Now, I realized that transitions can be painful. I had been lulled into a false sense of security because of my money, title and accomplishments. In my effort to do the work on myself that was needed after my loss and in my transition, I decided to reacquaint myself with some biblical transitions.

Biblical Transitions

David's Transition

David's transition began with the rejection of Saul by God, because of God Saul's disobedience. David was content taking care of his father's sheep, he was not looking for a promotion, and he was just a teenager. When God rejected Saul, He sent the prophet Samuel to anoint the new king. Samuel went to the family that God instructed him to go to but Samuel had no idea which of the sons was going to be anointed as king. When the prophet Samuel invited David's father Jesse and all of his sons to attend the sacrifice, David was not there, David was left in the field tending the sheep. What was it that caused David's father to not consider David to be worthy to attend the sacrifice?

> "And he said, peaceably: I am come to sacrifice unto the LORD: sanctify yourselves, and come with me to the sacrifice. And he sanctified Jesse and his sons, and called them to the sacrifice. And it came to pass, when they were come, that he looked on Eliab, and said, surely the LORD's anointed is before him. But the LORD said unto Samuel, Look not on his countenance, or on the height of his stature; because I have refused him: for the LORD seeth not as man seeth; for man looketh on the outward appearance, but the LORD looketh on the heart. Then Jesse called Abinadab, and made him pass before Samuel. And he said, neither hath the LORD chosen this. Then Jesse made Shammah to pass by. And he said, neither hath the LORD chosen this"~1 Samuel 16:5-13

David was content keeping his father's sheep. In the pasture he could compose and play his music, he could practice his skill with his sling shot. But most importantly, he could be in the presence of the Lord. On at least two occasions he defended the sheep against a dangerous predator, he killed a lion and a bear. The sheep didn't belong to him, they were his fathers but he risked his life to keep them safe.

> "Again, Jesse made seven of his sons to pass before Samuel. And Samuel said unto Jesse, The LORD hath not chosen these. 11 And Samuel said unto Jesse, Are here all thy children? And he said, There remaineth yet the youngest, and, behold, he keepeth the sheep. And Samuel said unto Jesse, Send and fetch him: for we will not sit down till he come hither. 12 And he sent, and brought him in. Now he was ruddy, and withal of a beautiful countenance, and goodly to look to. And the LORD said, Arise, anoint him: for this is he" ~I Samuel 16:10-12

After Samuel rejected all of Jesse's other sons and pressed the issue, David was brought in from the field. David made a significant transition that day because he was anointed king of Israel. I wonder what David thought about after being anointed. There was a period of time from the time he was anointed until he actually became the King but the day that he was anointed with oil he was also anointed with the Holy Spirit. David probably looked no different after Samuel anointed him but he entered a period of transition from that day. David returned to the field to continue caring for the sheep but his life was never the same.

> *"Then Samuel took the horn of oil, and anointed him in the midst of his brethren: and the Spirit of the LORD came upon David from that day forward. So Samuel rose up, and went to Ramah"* ~I Samuel 16:13

King Saul, the current king of Israel was undergoing a transition of his own. Just as the Holy Spirit came upon David, the Holy Spirit left King Saul and an evil spirit came upon him. Transitioning often occurs with positioning. When the evil spirit came upon King Saul the only way to sooth him was with music. Because David was noticed making music while in the field with the sheep, he was summoned to play music for King Saul. During this transition, two things happened David became a part-timed sheppard and a part-time musician and he also gained access to the palace, the place of his new assignment.

One day David's father called him in from the field to take food to his brothers who were with the army of Israel fighting the Philistines. David arrived just in time to hear the champion of the Philistines, Goliath, hurl insults against Israel. All of Israel, including King Saul was terrified of Goliath, but David immediately sized up the situation based on his past experiences, his knowledge and relationship with God. David offered to fight Goliath.

The man who could defeat Goliath would receive a bounty; his family would no longer have to pay taxes and he would marry the daughter of the king. David accepted the challenge. David used the crisis of this situation as his opportunity; it was a springboard that propelled him toward his destiny, it was a destiny moment, by choosing to fight the giant rather than minding his business and returning to the sheep as his brothers wanted, he ushered in another transition and he never returned to the sheep!

King Saul offered David his amour but David didn't accept the offer because the amour did not fit, he had not proved it, it was weighty and unfamiliar to him. Instead, he trusted in someone and something that was tried and true, he trusted in God! And he used something that had worked before, his sling shot. His defeat of the lion and the bear added to his confidence and he knew that God was with him as he had been before. King Saul's experience with David up to that time was that of a part time musician but he was about to see a different side of this young man.

"And David said to Saul, Let no man's heart fail because of him; thy servant will go and fight with this Philistine. And Saul said to David, Thou art not able to go against this Philistine to fight with him: for thou art but a youth, and he a man of war from his youth. And David said unto Saul, Thy servant kept his father's

> *sheep, and there came a lion, and a bear, and took a lamb out of the flock: And I went out after him, and smote him, and delivered it out of his mouth: and when he arose against me, I caught him by his beard, and smote him, and slew him. Thy servant slew both the lion and the bear: and this uncircumcised Philistine shall be as one of them, seeing he hath defied the armies of the living God"* ~1 Samuel 17:32-3

Have you ever fallen prey to someone else's expectation? It is unclear from the text what King Saul's expectations of David were; did he think that David would defeat Goliath? What is clear is that after Goliath's defeat, David and Saul's relationship also changed. With every victory that David had King Saul became increasingly hostile. Sometimes people are upset with you not because you did something wrong but because you did something right and although it may not be your intention to show them up, they perceive it that way.

Although David defeated Goliath he did not marry King Saul's elder daughter because King Saul gave her to someone else (broken promise). When King Saul did give David his younger daughter as a wife it wasn't because she would be a good wife but because Saul knew that she would be a snare to David. Eventually King Saul wanted David dead. When the people sang Saul has killed his thousand and David his ten thousand, it was more than King Saul could take.

> *"And Saul said to David, Behold my elder daughter Merab, her will I give thee to wife: only be thou valiant for me, and fight the LORD's battles. For Saul said, Let not mine hand be upon him, but let the hand of the Philistines be upon him. 18 And David said unto Saul, Who am I? And what is my life, or my father's family in Israel, that I should be son in law to the king? 19 But it came to pass at the time when Merab Saul's daughter should have been given to David that she was given unto Adriel the Meholathite to wife. 20 And Michal Saul's daughter loved David: and they told Saul, and the thing pleased him. 21 And Saul said, I will give him her, that she may be a snare to him, and that the hand of the Philistines may be against him. Wherefore Saul said to David, Thou shalt this day be my son in law in the one of the twain"* ~1 Samuel 18:17-21

King Saul saw the king in David without ever knowing that earlier Samuel the prophet had anointed David to be king of Israel, he sensed that it was only a matter of time. Sometimes people see in us what we fail to see in ourselves. If a person sees you in their position, that can cause a problem. David did everything that he could to convince King Saul of his loyalty but King Saul would not be convinced. King Saul realized that being king had very little to do with David and everything to do with what God wanted. Saul remembered how he had been chosen to become king.

Transitions are often found in unexpected events, like my being asked to relocate to Atlanta, GA. Some people call this "Kairos moments", the set or proper time. It is important to recognize "Kairos moments" because they are connected to opportunity and destiny. Decisions made at these moments are pivotal. For instance, if I had not decided to move (which I know was the right decision), I would not be writing this book nor would I have experienced all of the things that led up to its writing or other events that have taken place in my life.

Although David knew that one day he would be the king, he was never arrogant and he never disrespected King Saul even when King Saul pursued him to kill him. David always honored King Saul even when his actions were less than honorable because to David, King Saul was the anointed of the Lord. David faced hardship at the hands of King Saul until the Kings death.

> *"Now the Philistines fought against Israel: and the men of Israel fled from before the Philistines, and fell down slain in mount Gilboa. And the Philistines followed hard upon Saul and upon his sons; and the Philistines slew Jonathan, and Abinadab, and Melchishua, Saul's sons. And the battle went sore against Saul, and the archers hit him; and he was sore wounded of the archers. Then said Saul unto his armourbearer, Draw thy sword, and thrust me through therewith; lest these uncircumcised come and thrust me through, and abuse me. But his armour bearer would not; for he was sore afraid. Therefore Saul took a sword, and fell upon it"* ~1 Samuel 31:1-4

Jonathan, King Saul's son also recognized the king in David but he had a totally different attitude toward David.

Jonathan entered into covenant with David knowing that one day David would be King over Israel. Jonathan decided to help David. When you are in transition there is always someone there who will be helpful. I recall that when I was going through a very difficult time at work, one lady continued to be friendly and occasionally we had lunch together that small act of kindness made a big difference on some bad days.

Joseph's Transition

It is impossible to think about biblical transitions without thinking about Joseph. Joseph was given a dream as a youth that he didn't fully understand; when he told the dream to his family they became aggravated with him. When Joseph told his family about his dream, the content of the dream only served to alienate Joseph further from his already jealous brothers. Eventually, Joseph's brothers sold him into slavery and he was taken to Egypt as a slave. Sometimes transitions are about not only what you are called to do but where you are called to do it. In Egypt Joseph was sold to Potiphar and became Potiphar's overseer, Joseph was well liked and trusted and everything he puts his hands to prospered.

"And Joseph was brought down to Egypt; and Potiphar, an officer of Pharaoh, captain of the guard, an Egyptian, bought him of the hands of the Ishmeelites, which had brought him down thither. And the LORD was with Joseph, and he was a prosperous man;

> *and he was in the house of his master the Egyptian" ~Genesis 39:1-2*

For the first time since being sold into slavery, Joseph was comfortable in the service to Potiphar but another transition forced him to be in the right place at the right time because he had multiple transitions. Joseph diligently warded off the attempted seductions of Potiphar's wife but was still put in the jail after her false accusations (false accusations precede supernatural promotion). Joseph was truthful, he was honest, and he had done nothing to receive a jail sentence. We can be certain that Potiphar knew that Joseph was telling the truth because Joseph wasn't executed and he was placed in the royal prison.

I remember on one occasion my ex-manager's manager who at the time was the regional vice president had come to Atlanta. I knew him fairly well because we served together on the Diversity Council and he knew about the success of the projects that I worked on in the Council. We attended the same monthly all day meetings held in Charlotte, North Carolina and we had a fair amount of interaction. On this particular visit to our office, my manager, her manager and I sat down for a meeting. After the pleasantries were over we got down to business.

The business turned out to be me. My manager made some statements and took out a folder and gave the folder to her manager. As he listened to my manager's comments and read through the folder, suddenly he looked up at me and said to me "you and I serve on the Council together, I see and interact with you monthly, it's hard for me to believe that what I see here is about you." but like Potiphar, he choose to remain on the side of the accuser. I knew that he knew that the information was not true but by the end of the meeting he asked me if I would consider taking a demotion. I thought to myself "these people are crazy". When I told him "no" he asked me why, I looked him in the eye and told him "I had worked too hard to get where I was." The problem had nothing to do with my ability to do the job, which was later confirmed by Human Resources. For my manager, this was another one of her methods of intimidation and control; I'd seen her do it before. This meeting was a setup but I was not going backwards.

The question reminded me of a situation that a close friend of mine once faced, she was passed over for a promotion and when she inquired why, she was told by her manager that he didn't know that she wanted the promotion! Who doesn't want a promotion? She was already working in the position and had to train the new person for the position, why wouldn't she want it?

I had already seen my ex-manager unfairly demote a young lady who had gone along with it, she needed the job and she remained constantly under the thumb of my ex-manager, it was my ex-manager's way of maintaining control, which was not going to happen to me! I had already gone through the other manipulative tactics and this was just another ploy. For me at the time, keeping my title was more important than keeping my job. The title was more than initials behind my name; it represented everything that I had done through the years. There was a price that I had paid during the years and I was unwilling to give up or to relinquish anything based on the lies.

People in management and leadership positions make decisions for all types of reasons, some of which have nothing to do with the way a person is doing their job. Sometimes a decision is based on an alliance or an exchange of favors. Recently while I was riding in an elevator, two men got in the elevator and continued a discussion about how they needed to precede to release a woman from her job. I listened as they discussed how to strategically prevent her from keeping the job but somehow I knew that it wasn't personal, it was part of their job.

Potiphar knew Joseph's loyalty and he also knew his wife's character but in the end Joseph had to pay the price for Potiphar's decision. Although Joseph had done nothing wrong and had maintained his integrity, he was sentenced to prison.

Up until this time in the text we know that Joseph is a dreamer but we don't know that he has become an interpreter of the dreams of others. Joseph always acknowledged that it was God who interpreted dreams and he knew how to hear from God. Somewhere during the course of his hardships Joseph discovered and cultivated a skill or spiritual ability. When Pharaoh's cup bearer and baker were put into prison where Joseph was and he interpreted their dreams. Their dreams came true just as Joseph said that they would. Joseph asked the cup bearer to tell Pharaoh about him and how he interpreted their dreams. But, when the cup bearer was released from prison but it took him two years before he told Pharaoh about Joseph.

Can you imagine waiting two years hoping that today might be the day that I get out of prison? But Joseph was not idle during his time in prison; he was prosperous even in prison. Prosperity is not only money; after all money is only a means to obtain what you really want which are goods or services. If you get the goods or services without the money you're still prosperous? Prosperity also implies wellbeing.

> "And he asked Pharaoh's officers that were with him in the ward of his lord's house, saying, wherefore look ye so sadly to day? And they said unto him, we have dreamed a dream, and there is no interpreter of it. And Joseph said unto them, do not interpretations belong to God? Tell me them, I pray you. And the chief butler told his dream to Joseph, and said to him, In my dream, behold, a vine was before me; And in the vine were three branches: and it was as though it budded, and her blossoms shot forth; and the clusters thereof brought forth ripe grapes: And Pharaoh's cup was in my hand: and I took the grapes, and pressed them into Pharaoh's cup,

> *and I gave the cup into Pharaoh's hand. And Joseph said unto him, this is the interpretation of it: The three branches are three days: Yet within three days shall Pharaoh lift up thine head, and restore thee unto thy place: and thou shalt deliver Pharaoh's cup into his hand, after the former manner when thou wast his butler. But think on me when it shall be well with thee, and shew kindness, I pray thee, unto me, and make mention of me unto Pharaoh, and bring me out of this house: For indeed I was stolen away out of the land of the Hebrews: and here also have I done nothing that they should put me into the dungeon. When the chief baker saw that the interpretation was good, he said unto Joseph, I also was in my dream, and, behold, I had three white baskets on my head: And in the uppermost basket there was of all manner of bakemeats for Pharaoh; and the birds did eat them out of the basket upon my head. And Joseph answered and said, this is the interpretation thereof: The three baskets are three days: Yet within three days shall Pharaoh lift up thy head from off thee, and shall hang thee on a tree; and the birds shall eat thy flesh from off thee. And it came to pass the third day, which was Pharaoh's birthday that he made a feast unto all his servants: and he lifted up the head of the chief butler and of the chief baker among his servants. And he restored the chief butler unto his butlership again; and he gave the cup into Pharaoh's hand: But he hanged the chief baker: as Joseph had interpreted to them. Yet did not the chief butler remember Joseph, but forgat him" ~Genesis 40:7-23*

Pharaoh's cup bearer didn't remember Joseph until Pharaoh had a dream that no one could interpret. When Pharaoh learned of Joseph's ability to interpret dreams, he had Joseph brought to him. Before Joseph came to see Pharaoh, he cleaned, dressed and prepared for the meeting. Pharaoh may have never seen Joseph before but Joseph probably had seen Pharaoh before since he worked for Potiphar.

Joseph knew the Egyptian culture, including what was acceptable in Egyptian society. Joseph prepared himself to be presentable to Pharaoh. Pharaoh was the most sovereign authority over the land of Egypt. The first thing that Joseph did was to shave because Egyptians were clean shaven; Jews were not which was offensive to Egyptians. During Joseph's time in transition he prepared his manner of speech, his accumulation of knowledge and his mindset, he maintained a positive attitude although he was wrongfully accused and held in bondage.

When Pharaoh told Joseph his dream, Joseph didn't say "let me go pray about it," Joseph gave the interpretation right away. And then Joseph went a step further, he gave Pharaoh his resume. He told Pharaoh exactly what needed to be done knowing that there was no one in Egypt capable of doing the job but him. Essentially, Joseph gave Pharaoh a presentation of the problem and the solution. When Pharaoh listened to Joseph he realized that the only one capable of executing such a plan could only be the person who suggested the plan and Joseph got the job.

> *"Then Pharaoh sent and called Joseph, and they brought him hastily out of the dungeon: and he shaved himself, and changed his raiment, and came in unto Pharaoh. And Pharaoh said unto Joseph, I have dreamed a dream, and there is none that can*

interpret it: and I have heard say of thee, that thou canst understand a dream to interpret it. And Joseph answered Pharaoh, saying, It is not in me: God shall give Pharaoh an answer of peace. And Pharaoh said unto Joseph, In my dream, behold, I stood upon the bank of the river: And, behold, there came up out of the river seven kine, fatfleshed and well favoured; and they fed in a meadow: And, behold, seven other kine came up after them, poor and very ill favoured and leanfleshed, such as I never saw in all the land of Egypt for badness: And the lean and the ill favoured kine did eat up the first seven fat kine: And when they had eaten them up, it could not be known that they had eaten them; but they were still ill favoured, as at the beginning. So I awoke. And I saw in my dream, and, behold, seven ears came up in one stalk, full and good: And, behold, seven ears, withered, thin, and blasted with the east wind, sprung up after them: And the thin ears devoured the seven good ears: and I told this unto the magicians; but there was none that could declare it to me. And Joseph said unto Pharaoh, The dream of Pharaoh is one: God hath shewed Pharaoh what he is about to do. The seven good kine are seven years; and the seven good ears are seven years: the dream is one. And the seven thin and ill favoured kine that came up after them are seven years; and the seven empty ears blasted with the east wind shall be seven years of famine. This is the thing which I have spoken unto Pharaoh: What God is about to do he sheweth unto Pharaoh. Behold, there come seven years of great plenty throughout all the land of Egypt: And there shall arise after them seven years of famine; and all the plenty shall be forgotten in the land of Egypt; and the famine shall consume the land; And the plenty shall not be known in the land by reason of that famine following; for it shall be very grievous. And for that the dream was doubled unto Pharaoh twice; it is because the thing is established by God, and God will shortly bring it to pass. Now therefore let Pharaoh look out a man discreet and wise, and set him over the land of Egypt. Let Pharaoh do this, and let him appoint officers over the land, and take up the fifth part of the land of Egypt in the seven plenteous years. And let them gather all

> the food of those good years that come, and lay up corn under the hand of Pharaoh, and let them keep food in the cities. And that food shall be for store to the land against the seven years of famine, which shall be in the land of Egypt; that the land perish not through the famine. And the thing was good in the eyes of Pharaoh, and in the eyes of all his servants. And Pharaoh said unto his servants, Can we find such a one as this is, a man in whom the Spirit of God is? And Pharaoh said unto Joseph, Forasmuch as God hath shewed thee all this, there is none so discreet and wise as thou art: Thou shalt be over my house, and according unto thy word shall all my people be ruled: only in the throne will I be greater than thou. And Pharaoh said unto Joseph, See, I have set thee over all the land of Egypt. And Pharaoh took off his ring from his hand, and put it upon Joseph's hand, and arrayed him in vestures of fine linen, and put a gold chain about his neck" ~Genesis 41:14-42

Pharaoh recognized an articulate, knowledgeable, well dressed, man full of wisdom, an interpreter of dreams. Pharaoh took the ring from his hand and put it on Joseph's hand (and it fit!) signifying that there was no one in the land higher than Joseph except for Pharaoh and then Pharaoh gave Joseph a new name, Zaphnath-paaneah, one who discovers hidden things.

Each time that Joseph encountered a transition he grew from the experience and each transition prepared and positioned him for his destiny. Although he went through many painful events, he ended up at the right place at the right time. For me, going through the transitions after my job loss was exciting and scary. I had always been successful in my career; I had always gone the extra mile to secure knowledge and credentials to evidence my level of expertise in the field. I had also done a lot of personal development and training so that I would be well rounded. When I thought about it, I had been in preparation for this transition for a long time.

It took faith to pursue the vision that God had given me. Many of the decisions that I made took me further out of my comfort zone. Every activity that In His Season, Inc. did was a complete act of faith. God began to bring people into my life that could help me with the vision and I continued to build and to pursue His direction for my life. Just as Potiphor's wife was instrumental to Joseph's destiny, my ex-manager was instrumental to my life taking the direction toward my destiny.

The things that happened to me were just shifts in my life. I realized that everything in my life up to that point lead to my job loss, it was not one incident but a series of events; my birth, my education, my life circumstances, my beliefs, my core values and my decisions. I had become a vice president by the grace of God. Yes, I had put in a lot of hard work, but when it really came down to it, it was God who had called the shots all along.

He opened doors and gave me favor the right relationships crossed my path. In the beginning of my career, all I wanted to be was a Corporate Trust

Administrator. God took my career much further than I dreamed or imagined that it would go. Just as He had blessed me before He wanted to bless me again. God's intent is always to bless us no matter how dire the circumstance may seem. He loves us with a love that cannot be described.

Part III

CHAPTER 7

Understanding What You Have Learned

Some people would have been able to accept what happened and simply would have moved on with their life. For me that was not the case, I realized that part of my journey was to get a full understanding of the situation and to pass that information on, that was part of my assignment. Many people are faced with loss of one kind or another for me it was the loss of a career. God doesn't do things haphazardly, there is always a reason although sometimes it may not make total sense to us at first but there is usually an "Aha" moment, a time when the light of our understanding comes on and we understand.

The layers of my life had been peeled away like the layers of an onion. Each layer revealed a different layer until finally the core was reached. Now, a rebuilding could take place from the inside out. It was like being born again, again with renewed understanding of God and His ways.

I began to see that God had begun to prepare me even before I left New York. For more than six months He had me meditate in the book of Joshua. I didn't know why I could not stop reading that book. The revelation that I got from reading the book was that to be strong and courageous was not a suggestion, it was a command. There were other things like dreams and at the time, I didn't understand the significance or meaning.

Each decade of my life was so diverse and so different from the last that I had potential to relate to the needs of many different people. People now have so many needs. Our world is in transition our economy and governing bodies throughout the world are all in transition.

Moral decline and the breakdown of the family unit are the order of the day. It's not that the world has not seen this type of decline before because it has. I laugh when people say that they wish that they had lived during Jesus' time; I wonder have they looked around! Do they realize that we live in a generation where the gospel is virtually unknown by most unbelievers and unfortunately some believers. If you read the book of Romans you will see where the apostle Paul addressed the gentile church about some of the same things we see today. We are living in the times like Jesus's time.

In I Kings we can read about a transition in power and authority that I also believe is similar to the times that we live in.

> "And he came thither unto a cave, and lodged there; and, behold, the word of the LORD came to him, and he said unto him, what doest thou here, Elijah? And he said I have been very jealous for the LORD God of hosts: for the children of Israel have forsaken thy covenant, thrown down thine altars, and slain thy prophets with the sword; and I, even I only, am left; and they seek my life, to take it away. And he said, Go forth, and stand upon the mount before the LORD. And, behold, the LORD passed by, and a great and strong wind rent the mountains, and brake in pieces the rocks before the LORD; but the LORD was not in the wind: and after the wind an earthquake; but the LORD was not in the earthquake: And after the earthquake a fire; but the LORD was not in the fire: and after the fire a still small voice.
>
> And it was so, when Elijah heard it, that he wrapped his face in his mantle, and went out, and stood in the entering in of the cave. And, behold, there came a voice unto him, and said, what doest thou here, Elijah? And he said, I have been very jealous for the LORD God of hosts: because the children of Israel have forsaken thy covenant, thrown down thine altars, and slain thy prophets with the sword; and I, even I only, am left; and they seek my life, to take it away. And the LORD said unto him, Go, return on thy way to the wilderness of Damascus: and when thou comest, anoint Hazael to be king over Syria: And Jehu the son of Nimshi shalt thou anoint to be king over Israel: and Elisha the son of Shaphat of Abelmeholah shalt thou anoint to be prophet in thy room. And it shall come to pass,

> *that him that escapeth the sword of Hazael shall Jehu slay: and him that escapeth from the sword of Jehu shall Elisha slay.*
>
> *Yet I have left me seven thousand in Israel, all the knees which have not bowed unto Baal, and every mouth which hath not kissed him"* ~1 Kings 19:9-18

Elijah had a tremendous victory but immediately afterwards experienced a time of fear and hiding. Elijah thought that he was alone and that no other believers remained but God let him know that was not true. God had kept seven thousand faithful believers. Elijah's words demonstrate his feeling of hopelessness, he repeats how Israel has sinned and boasted of his actions for the Lord (he mentions it twice!) but he was hiding!

In our times when it seems that God is losing, He is not losing at all. God is raising up believers like those in Jesus' time, a generation of believers who have not been compromised and are not hindered by the traditions of men. Like the transition of the passing of the mantle from Elijah to Elisha, there is an overlap of chosen people for a period of time. This next generation of believers will not hide but will do twice as much!

The "ah ha" moment for me was when I realized that Corporate Trust was not the reason that God opened the door for me to move to Atlanta. I had been in prayer for some time because of the extensive change that the industry that I worked in was undergoing. They were pioneering a new way of doing the business and I didn't like the new structure. I knew that I did not want to work within the new structure.

I had been asking God in prayer what I was to do. The day that I was asked about moving to the new office in Atlanta, I knew it was the answer to my prayers; the Atlanta office would not undergo the new structure for at least two years. I didn't know what would happen after the two years but I knew it was only a matter of time before other banks used the new structure too. I didn't know at the time that my life was going through a shift that would change the entire direction of my life.

Now that the shift had taken place, my life took on a totally new direction. I realized what all the craziness was about. I arrived at this new direction not through a change of my mind but through the arm of adversity. Like Joseph, David and others in the bible, adversity was at the crossroad of my life and was necessary for me to reach my destiny.

Reading bible stories is not the same as experiencing bible truths. The pattern that emerged from my meditation in the book of Joshua was not only to have courage but also to prepare for the giants! I didn't know that the giants were not only external but also internal; I learned that the failures in life are as significant as the successes.

I believe that this generation will not only read the bible stories but they will also experience the truths. The interesting thing is that I'm not alone in this type of transition. There are ministers leaving ministry and entering into business, business people leaving business entering ministry. Transition is everywhere. Employees are leaving jobs and embracing the call to entrepreneurship. I believe that all of this movement is being orchestrated by God. My point is that things are in a state of change and may not make sense in the natural but in the spirit realm they make sense.

I had no real desire to leave Corporate Trust but after a period of time, I realized that my life had become stagnant. With the changes coming to the industry, I knew that I would not like it. The job loss forced me to not only examine myself but also to explore the many changes in technology, information and systems. I had an excitement with each new discovery especially when that discovery was able to help others. It was fun planning strategy for the company, writing articles, meeting new people and discussing their visions.

My goal to train and develop people how to navigate in this new world took on significance. Where the church has trained people in spiritual matters it lacks knowledge concerning business, technology, media and other aspects of today's world. It is no longer church as usual. The church needs business and business needs the church.

I believe that tools like the internet, multimedia, social networks, books, and other resources have been placed in the world to be used by the church to accomplish God's agenda. Churches and individuals who try to fight against the technology tide will be swept away. Those that view the changes as being "not of God" don't understand that God creates while satan perverts, the first instruction of God has not changed, man is to have dominion. The church's assignment has not changed, we are to go into the entire world and preach the gospel, but the methods to reach the world have changed.

I seldom look back now, when I do I think of my ex-manager as an instrument that was used to move me into my future. I know that I have not fully arrived at what God has for me, but now I can laugh at the situation and I realize that I'm in a much better place now, in the will of God. I think differently about a lot of things and I can now use the skills that I learned in Corporate America to further the Kingdom of God.

Nowadays it's all about what God wants. I graduated from ministry school and now I'm a licensed minister although my assignment is more marketplace. I know that my assignment is not the four walls of the church or the pulpit ministry and it's also not a street ministry. What God has assigned to me is more digital, internet, informational, training and development business/ministry, writing, speaking and coaching. I know that's a mouth full! It's different. It took me a while to understand exactly what God had in mind.

I was blessed to have a career in Corporate Trust that I loved so much (maybe too much) that I didn't want to let it go but now I know that God was leading me on a path that would give me even more joy. Not only will it bring me joy but it will also help others on their journey.

God loved me so much that He did not allow me to stay in my comfort zone. During a time when the world is in the most important change that it has ever been in, I have been positioned to be a blessing. When I prayed about what to do next about the changes on my job, I could never have imagined that God would use this as an opportunity to change my entire life. The funny thing is that God did not spare me the pain of change; He simply loved me through each painful event. He prepared me at times when I allowed Him to and in times when I resisted and could not hear His voice, He allowed the friction to shape me. As Jesus told Paul in the book of Acts "It is hard to kick against the pricks."

> "And thou shalt remember all the way which the LORD thy God led thee these forty years in the wilderness, to humble thee, and to prove thee, to know what was in thine heart, whether thou wouldest keep his commandments, or no" ~Deuteronomy 8:2

I would have loved to reach where I am today without going through what I had to go through but, looking back, I realize that for me somewhere along the way, I would have had to deal with the areas in my life at another time.

I'm glad that the unfortunate course of events allowed me to deal with these areas in my life in depth at this stage of the journey. I know that there are areas in my life where there may always be an internal struggle but because I am aware of them the enemy can no longer use them as he once did.

I am satisfied that I have reached the level of awareness needed to serve as a foundation for my continued growth. Through the adversity, I am more knowledgeable and stronger than I was before. My relationship with God is stronger. My insight about other people, their needs and circumstances are much better.

I encountered every aspect of myself on this portion of my journey including those aspects that I didn't want to admit existed, the good the bad and the ugly. I ran into the fool, the double minded person, the forgetful hearer, and the fearful person. The enemy usedpersecution, isolation, accusation, loss, fear, doubt, and discouragement but in the end, God helped me to pass every test.

Some people only tell the parts of their testimony that they believe people can handle and using wisdom is always good. Transparency is difficult especially for leaders, there is an expectation of perfection but I believe that if we allow more transparent testimonies, we will all profit from the experience of others.

The truth is that we need to share testimonies, the things that we discover in our own Christian journey, good or bad.

Man is a spirit who lives in a body and processes a soul, the soul of man has three components; the mind, the will and the emotions. All three of these work together but because they are not renewed instantly at the new birth, they must be taught and trained by the Word and the Holy Spirit. The body also has to be trained but is only capable of carrying out the dictates of the spirit and the soul. The dictionary definition of the mind will and emotions are listed here:

<u>Mind</u>

The human consciousness that originates in the brain and is manifested esp. in thought, memory, perception, feeling, will or imagination.

Will
The mental faculty by which one deliberately chooses or decides on a course of action: Volition.

Emotions
A complex, usually strong subjective response, as love or fear; such a response involving psychological changes as a preparation for action; the part of the consciousness that involves feeling or sensibility.

The mind reasons, the will chooses and the emotions feel. Although these three can be defined separately they are really intertwined and impact one another. Sometimes the emotions win over the good sense of the mind but for a Christian, the re-born spirit should dominate over a renewed mind and a submitted soul.

Lessons and Principles Learned

God will prove those He loves.

Prove:

To learn or find out by experience: to test the truth, validity, or genuineness of: to test the worth or quality of; *specifically*: to compare against a standard. The Merriam-Webster Online Dictionary. 2009

Exodus 16:4
Then said the LORD unto Moses, Behold, I will rain bread from heaven for you; and the people shall go out and gather a certain rate every day, that I may prove them, whether they will walk in my law, or no.

Judges 2:22
That through them I may prove Israel, whether they will keep the way of the LORD to walk therein, as their fathers did keep it, or not.

Judges 3:1
Now these are the nations which the LORD left, to prove Israel by them, even as many of Israel as had not known all the wars of Canaan;

Judges 3:4
And they were to prove Israel by them, to know whether they would hearken unto the commandments of the LORD, which he commanded their fathers by the hand of Moses.

Psalm 26:2

Examine me, O LORD, and prove me; try my reins and my heart

1 Thessalonians 5:21
Prove all things; hold fast that which is good.

Each level of Christian growth requires a test (proving).
- All testing is based on resistance.
- The test is an open book test (requires your knowledge of the Word).
- You cannot pass the test using the same information that caused the test.
- Each test leaves you on a higher level once you pass the test.
- If you qualify, you can skip the test

Open Doors

Disobedience will open the door to the enemy, all disobedience is wrong regardless of the reason. In my opinion, there are basically three types of Disobedience:

- Ignorance (You don't know that you are being disobedient, you lack knowledge).

- Stupidity (You allow your emotions to override your obedience and your good sense).
- Blatant disregard (you know but you don't care, rebellion).
-

As I heard one speaker's quote "if you think education is expensive try ignorance."

God Uses Opportunity for Kingdom Business

Times of Incubation are times of development; these times require a certain environment to produce the correct product. Lemons only produce lemon juice when they are placed into an environment where they are squeezed. The four stages of metamorphosis that a caterpillar goes through to become a butterfly are its incubation stages but it is also the period of struggle to escape its captivity that develops the butterfly's wings which enables it to fly.

I know now that not only did God want me to trust Him at a higher level, it was also the other way around! He trusted me to go through everything that I went through and to remain faithful to Him.

I had become complacent, content and comfortable in my career, I thought that was it for me, I didn't see anything more beyond where I was. I had not come close to the destiny that God had for me. Without the interruption to my life at a magnitude sufficient to dislodge me from an apathetic place that was so much less than what God saw for me. He loved me too much to let me stay as I was.

> *"My brethren, count it all joy when ye fall into divers temptations; Knowing this, that the trying of your faith worketh patience. But let patience have her perfect work, that ye may be perfect and entire, wanting nothing" ~James 1:2-4*

One of the greatest examples of how people make the transition from where they are now to where they are going is the story of the exodus of the children of Israel from Egypt to Canaan. The account depicts all of the frailties of human nature when faced with change. There is the tendency to question how you got to where you are, to murmur and complain, to want to return to the familiar and to repeat mistakes.

The story of the Exodus from Egypt doesn't start with Mosses it starts with Joseph. You won't appreciate the way out until you remember the way in. The children of Israel came to Egypt in a time of famine. Joseph had gained prominence and asked Pharaoh's permission for his family to join him there. The children of Israel were in Egypt because Joseph had favor with Pharaoh, initially they were treated well

"Then Joseph came and told Pharaoh, and said, My father and my brethren, and their flocks, and their herds, and all that they have, are come out of the land of Canaan; and, behold, they are in the land of Goshen. And he took some of his brethren, even five men, and presented them unto Pharaoh. And Pharaoh said unto his brethren, what is your occupation? And they said unto Pharaoh, Thy servants are shepherds, both we, and also our fathers. They said morever unto Pharaoh, For to sojourn in the land are we come; for thy servants have no pasture for their flocks; for the famine is sore in the land of Canaan: now therefore, we pray thee, let thy servants dwell in the land of Goshen. And Pharaoh spake unto Joseph, saying, Thy father and thy brethren are come unto thee: The land of Egypt is before thee; in the best of the land make thy father and brethren to dwell; in the land of Goshen let them dwell: and if thou knowest any men of activity among them, then make them rulers over my cattle. And Joseph brought in Jacob his father, and set him before Pharaoh: and Jacob blessed Pharaoh. And Pharaoh said unto Jacob, How old art thou? And Jacob said unto Pharaoh, The days of the years of my pilgrimage are an hundred and thirty years: few and evil have the days of the years of my life been, and have not attained unto the days of the years of the life of my fathers in the days of their pilgrimage. And Jacob blessed Pharaoh, and went out from before Pharaoh. And Joseph placed his father and his brethren, and gave them a possession in the land of Egypt, in the best of the land, in the land of Rameses, as Pharaoh had commanded"~Genesis 47: 1-11

Human nature is to stay in a place of comfort too long. Although scripture does not mention another leader of the children of Israel until Moses emerges to lead them out of Egypt, someone should have recognized that it was time to go. When things began to change around them and they had fallen out of favor it was time to go. Sometimes the only deliverer that you need is prayer. The bible says that they cried and their cry came up unto God by reason of the bondage

> "Now there arose up a new king over Egypt, which knew not Joseph. And he said unto his people, Behold, the people of the children of Israel are more and mightier than we: Come on, let us deal wisely with them; lest they multiply, and it come to pass, that, when there falleth out any war, they join also unto our enemies, and fight against us, and so get them up out of the land. Therefore they did set over them taskmasters to afflict them with their burdens. And they built for Pharaoh treasure cities, Pithom and Raamses. But the more they afflicted them, the more they multiplied and grew. And they were grieved because of the children of Israel. And the Egyptians made the children of Israel to serve with rigour: And they made their lives bitter with hard bondage, in morter, and in brick, and in all manner of service in the field: all their service, wherein they made them serve, was with rigour. And the king of Egypt spake to the Hebrew midwives, of which the name of the one was Shiphrah, and the name of the other Puah: And he said, When ye do the office of a midwife to the Hebrew women, and see them upon the stools; if it be a son, then ye shall kill him: but if it be a daughter, then she shall live. But the midwives feared God, and did not as the king of Egypt commanded them, but saved the men children alive" ~Exodus 1:8-17

Things changed drastically for the children of Israel but they continued to stay in their comfort zone. I know that it was the same way for me! I continued to want stay in the last place where the Lord had blessed me even when it was obvious that the plan had shifted. Fear will cause you to sit back while faith will move you forward. Recognizing when to move is critical to God's plan for your life.

By that time Moses had gone through his own wilderness experience he was ready to return to Egypt to help to free the children of Israel. Until he confronted his own inadequacies and discovered God for himself, he couldn't help anyone else. Moses had an identity crisis; he didn't know who he was!

When Moses had become an adult, he searched out the Hebrews because he was reminded all of his life that he didn't fit in. After he killed an Egyptian and then became aware that there were witnesses, he had to flee into Median. Although Median was a place where he felt that he belonged, it was not where his destiny lied.

> *"And Moses was content to dwell with the man: and he gave Moses Zipporah his daughter. And she bare him a son, and he called his name Gershom: for he said, I have been a stranger in a strange land" ~Exodus 2:21-22*

We all want comfort and sameness but God calls each of us to be different. It is our differences that enable us to make the contribution that is needed in someone else's life. It took a God encounter for Moses to know his true value and even then he felt uncertain and unsure of himself but he knew that he could trust God. Since going through my own wilderness experience and fighting the giant, I learned several other things of importance: I learned how to fight and I learned when and when not to fight.

> *"Finally, my brethren, be strong in the Lord, and in the power of his might. Put on the whole armour of God, that ye may be able to stand against the wiles of the devil. For we wrestle not against flesh and blood, but against principalities, against powers, against the rulers of the darkness of this world, against spiritual wickedness in high places. Wherefore take unto you the whole armour of God, that ye may be able to withstand in the evil day, and having done all, to stand. Stand therefore, having your loins girt about with truth, and having on the breastplate of righteousness; And your feet shod with the preparation of the gospel of peace; Above all, taking the shield of faith, wherewith ye shall be able to quench all the fiery darts of the wicked. And take the helmet of salvation, and the sword of the Spirit, which is the word of God: Praying always with all prayer and supplication in the Spirit, and watching thereunto with all perseverance and supplication for all saints"*
> ~Ephesians 6: 10-18

You can't fight when you are not walking in love. It is too easy to blame people when people are not the enemy. Although the enemy will use people, it is important to focus on the promise and not on the problem. Kingdom principals always win! Don't talk about or discuss the problem instead talk about the goodness of God and meditate on scriptures based on where you're going and not where you are. Below is some kingdom fighting principles:

Bless them that curse you

Do good to them that hate you

Pray for them which despitefully use you, and persecute you

Do not render evil for evil, or railing for railing: but contrariwise blessing; knowing that ye are thereunto called, that ye should inherit a blessing.

> *"For though we walk in the flesh, we do not war after the flesh: (For the weapons of our warfare are not carnal, but mighty through God to the pulling down of strong holds; Casting down imaginations, and every high thing that exalteth itself against the knowledge of God, and bringing into captivity every thought to the obedience of Christ" ~II Corinthians 10:3-5*

These are all very basic Christian principles drawn directly from scripture. I remember when I was very young in the Lord someone gave me a pamphlet titled "Have You Left Your First Love" being young in the Lord, I didn't realize that as the Christian walk progresses the basics have to continually be reinforced. Our fight is continual so we must continually meditate in the basics of the Word of God to reinforce it in our lives. When we think that we already know this or that, we are in danger of being deceived by the enemy. The Word of God and the Holy Spirit is the only compass that we have to show us the way. When we seek the approval of man, we have been deceived. Not everything that appears right is right and not everything that appears wrong is wrong. Everything must be proved by the Word of God and the Holy Spirit. Even a Rhema Word from the Holy Spirit will line up with the written word!

For many years we have fallen short of the things that Jesus intends for us. We have viewed our faith through the eyes of denominationalism, traditions and twentieth and twenty first century social norms. These include our individual family values and our own individual beliefs but God intends for us to live not by these things but in spite of them. God intends that we seek first the Kingdom of God and His righteousness. We are in many ways like the people of Israel during King Josiah's time in II Chronicles 34: 1- 33, we need to rediscover what God has said and then do it.

We are living in a time when God is opening our eyes as never before. God is moving and shifting people to roles that they never intended to be in and to locations where they never intended to be. We have thought that anything that happens to us that seems hurtful is the devil but I found through my experiences that God uses the avenues that are available to Him. Let me clarify, God does not use satan's tactics which is anything that comes into our life to steal, to kill or to destroy; things intended to destroy you are not God. God's aim is to turn the situation around for our good. We see Him do this in the life of David, Joseph and Moses. God will use situations caused by our own ignorance or disobedience to instruct us. The ideal situation is that we do our homework and study the Word diligently. When we study His word and seek Him through the reading and meditation of His Word, we become intimately acquainted with His Spirit; we can bypass some of life's difficult lessons. God does not use sickness, disease, starvation and poverty to teach us anything but when we are in these types of situations; He will give us grace to come through them.

When God instructs us to seek first the kingdom of God, many of us have no concept of what Kingdom of God is! Jesus taught many principles about the Kingdom of God. Many of His parables dealt with the Kingdom of God. If we look at some of Jesus' actions, we can see the things that the Kingdom of God produces; He healed the sick, raised the dead, and got money from places that no one could have imagined like out of a fish's mouth!

This has to be explained because many times people don't know who is attacking them! They think that God is punishing them for some wrong that they have done but they are reaping what they have sown. God's punishment is not to be compared to His wrath or an attack of the enemy.

As more and more people began to pursue their God given destiny and purpose, it is unrealistic to believe that there will not be opposition. But opposition is only one aspect of pursuing destiny there are also lessons that need to be learned. These lessons are for the preparation for the future. Pursuing destiny is a faith walk. You may only have bits and pieces of information about your vision and dream. You may not be the person that you need to be for the future that God has planned for you. As you press toward your destiny you become a new person. The situations and circumstances that you encounter; new relationships, new information and new revelation reveal little by little the person who you are becoming.

It is His Word and the presence of the Holy Spirit that truly makes the difference. No matter how much you learn, the people you know or the talent that you have, as you pursue your destiny, you will need God's super on your natural!

Dr. Myles Monroe has authored several books about the Kingdom; the timing of these writing is no coincidence. As the world system suffers through many woes, God is reminding His people that we are dual citizens and that He is our source and that we are to live by Kingdom principles.

While going through the loss of my career and the many challenges that followed, I had to change. I had to surrender my will for His will. I had to begin to become the person that God saw when He looked at me. I had to embrace the call that God had placed on my life. My life did not change overnight in fact at times some things seemed to become more difficult. Navigating through the difficulties is part of the walk of faith.

For a period of time I enlisted the services of a Christian Life Coach to help me sort things out and to get my bearings. I read books like Failing Forward by John C. Maxwell to help deal with the feeling of failure. I had to accept my failure and realize that failure was not the end. The books that I read helped me to move forward through this period. I began to realize that failure is the part of success that most successful people don't discuss. Having faith doesn't prevent failure; having faith helps you to go through the failures realizing that something better is coming.

There are not many successful people who do not have failure somewhere in their history. The real test is will you look past the failure and pursue your destiny? Will you allow the mistakes to become your stepping stones? Will you allow the setback to become your setup for a comeback, as author and speaker Dr. Willie Jolley writes about?

I thank God for His faithfulness! He has shown me that through it all He is faithful. If God has given you a vision for your future there will be challenges before you see it come to pass. The hardest thing is to stay focused and to stay your course through the test and trials that come to thwart God's plans for you. It is important for you to remember that to every conclusion there is a beginning.

Very few people make it to the promise land without going through the wilderness and fighting the giants. There are things to conquer in the promise land and sometimes the enemy is without and at other times the enemy is within but God is unchanging. He is the GPS that will help you to navigate and find your way when life changes suddenly.

CHAPTER 8

New Beginnings

I've changed much since the event that caused my life to go in a different direction and I'm still changing. In every change God has proven His word over and over again. As I move forward toward my destiny, I am persuaded that God will never fail to fulfill every promise. Now I really know what success is. To be totally submitted to God is success. Someone once said that "life is like an onion, you have to peal it one layer at a time and sometimes you cry."

Many people are crying now because of loss especially job loss. Some have loss jobs because of the economy and others because of office politics and bad bosses but whatever the reason, God can take that loss and cause it to be the best thing that ever happened to you. God has a plan and purpose for your life. Although what you face may seem impossible, with God all things are possible. You may not have to look as deeply as I had to look to get to the root of the situation but, once you do find the root, quickly give the situation to God; cast all of your cares over on Him. If you need to repent, then repent and move forward with your life trusting that God is faithful.

All along the way in my journey God has provided people, resources and direction. If someone had said that I was going to be a published author and a licensed minister when I left the bank, I would have said "no way" but today, it's true. I was blessed before, but now I am also a blessing. God has a way of bringing the best out of some of the worst situations. When we get in step with His plan, we can't go wrong. Is it painful at times? Yes, but as you move forward His plan is revealed more and more. You begin to realize that His dream is bigger than yours. Right now you may be like Gideon, hiding out, but God will come where you are.

Gideon's Transition

> "And there came an angel of the LORD, and sat under an oak which was in Ophrah, that pertained unto Joash the Abiezrite: and his son Gideon threshed wheat by the winepress, to hide it from the Midianites. And the angel of the LORD appeared unto him, and said unto him, The LORD is with thee, thou mighty man of valour" ~Judges 6:11-12

God will come where you are and declare who you are. Gideon did not see himself as a mighty man of valor but God did. Gideon was hiding when God revealed His plan for him. The call of God was truly the beginning for Gideon because although he had knowledge about God; he really didn't know God. Gideon had become comfortable hiding out in a place where he believed he had no choice but to be because he was surrounded by the enemy.

God knew that He had called Gideon to save Israel but Gideon had such poor self-esteem that God infused him with confidence by calling him a "mighty man of valor." The baggage from Gideon's past crippled his capacity to see who he really was. God had to get Gideon to a place where new information was given to him that enabled him to reach forward to his future.

> "And the LORD looked upon him, and said, Go in this thy might, and thou shalt save Israel from the hand of the Midianites: have not I sent thee? And he said unto him, Oh my Lord, wherewith shall I save Israel? behold, my family is poor in Manasseh, and I am the least in my father's house. And the LORD said unto him, surely I will be with thee, and thou shalt smite the Midianites as one man" ~Judges 6:14-17

When Gideon heard God's vision for him, he moved forward. Although everything was not easy to do, Gideon followed God's directions even when it did not make sense. However, in the beginning, Gideon did not always act right away because of a lack of faith in God. Gideon asked that God prove His power several times to display that He was God. God accommodated Gideon and Gideon began to move into his destiny. Everything was not perfect and some of the instructions that Gideon was given were strange like reducing the number of men in his army before a battle.

> "And the LORD looked upon him, and said, go in this thy might, and thou shalt save Israel from the hand of the Midianites: have not I sent thee? And he said unto him, Oh my Lord, wherewith shall I save Israel? behold, my family is poor in Manasseh, and I am the least in my father's house. And the LORD said unto him, surely I will be with thee, and thou shalt smite the Midianites as one man" ~Judges 6:14-17

> "And the LORD said unto Gideon, The people that are with thee are too many for me to give the Midianites into their hands, lest Israel vaunt themselves against me, saying, Mine own hand hath saved me" ~Judges 7:2

I know firsthand that everything will not make sense. Most of the things that I encountered did not make a lot of sense to me at the time but I knew that God was in it. To go from a successful career to persecution and loss was not the road to the future that I would have willingly chosen. As I look at it now in retrospect, I am able to give God the praise for seeing something in me that at the time I did not see in myself. I am thankful that He did not leave me as I was. In many ways I am much better now. I'm better prepared to encourage others to pursue their God given destiny and to help them make it through the transitions that will take place along the way.

Moving through the roadblocks and the obstacles is not easy but, if you have the correct perspective it is extremely rewarding. As I continued to work on my dream with whatever resources were available and at times there weren't a lot of resources, God provided for me and my family. The only description that will fit the strategy for the continued building of the company is the story of Nehemiah building the wall.

Every progression in the building of my company has come at the same time that I faced great difficulty. I learned something about God; He can do more with less in lean times. You can't stop working diligently toward your goals even when finances and other resources seem limited and as you build you must also defend what you've already built.

> *"Now it came to pass when Sanballat, and Tobiah, and Geshem the Arabian, and the rest of our enemies, heard that I had builded the wall, and that there was no breach left therein; (though at that time I had not set up the doors upon the gates;) That Sanballat and Geshem sent unto me, saying, Come, let us meet together in some one of the villages in the plain of Ono. But they thought to do me mischief. And I sent messengers unto them, saying, I am doing a great work, so that I cannot come*

> *down: why should the work cease, whilst I leave it, and come down to you? Yet they sent unto me four times after this sort; and I answered them after the same manner"* ~Nehemiah 6:1-4

Nehemiah had a desire to return to Jerusalem and to rebuild the walls, even after he was given the resources he faced opposition but his attitude was to not stop the building but to continue building even in the face of adversity. At times the defense of the dream is equally important as the building of the dream.

> *"Therefore set I in the lower places behind the wall, and on the higher places, I even set the people after their families with their swords, their spears, and their bows. And I looked, and rose up, and said unto the nobles, and to the rulers, and to the rest of the people, be not ye afraid of them: remember the LORD, which is great and terrible, and fight for your brethren, your sons, and your daughters, your wives, and your houses. And it came to pass, when our enemies heard that it was known unto us, and God had brought their counsel to nought, that we returned all of us to the wall, every one unto his work. And it came to pass from that time forth, that the half of my servants wrought in the work, and the other half of them held both the spears, the shields, and the bows, and the habergeons; and the rulers were behind all the house of Judah. They which builded on the wall, and they that bare burdens, with those that laded, every one with one of his hands wrought in the work, and with the other hand held a weapon. For the builders, every one had his sword girded by his side, and so builded. And he that sounded the trumpet was by me"* ~Nehemiah 4:13-18

Building and defending go hand in hand. Whenever God gives you a dream there will be opposition but if you keep the right attitude God will do exactly what He said He would. He will bring you out of the adversity and direct you toward your future.

What an amazing time it is when you begin to focus on and move toward your purpose. Everything may not go perfectly and there will be challenges along the way but as you move forward the dream gets bigger and clearer. Some doors will open as others will close but you must maintain your focus on what God told you. Even the people who you felt would be supportive may not be supportive but God will always confirm His word.

At each level of your Christian growth you will encounter things to overcome. Many Christians think that they should not look back based on Philippians 3:13 but When Paul is speaking he is saying that he has made a choice not to focus on his past. He knows who he is as he clearly states in Philippians 3:2-8, he knew exactly who he was and what his past was. It might sound contradictory if not understood.

> "Brethren, I count not myself to have apprehended: but this one thing I do, forgetting those things which are behind, and reaching forth unto those things which are before" ~Philippians 3:13

> *"For we are the circumcision, which worship God in the spirit, and rejoice in Christ Jesus, and have no confidence in the flesh. Though I might also have confidence in the flesh. If any other man thinketh that he hath whereof he might trust in the flesh, I more: Circumcised the eighth day, of the stock of Israel, of the tribe of Benjamin, an Hebrew of the Hebrews; as touching the law, a Pharisee; Concerning zeal, persecuting the church; touching the righteousness which is in the law, blameless. But what things were gain to me, those I counted loss for Christ. Yea doubtless, and I count all things but loss for the excellency of the knowledge of Christ Jesus my Lord: for whom I have suffered the loss of all things, and do count them but dung, that I may win Christ"* ~Philippians 3:3-8

I'm sure that Paul had areas in his life that he had to deal with. I'm sure that he had a time of reflection and self-examination before he discovered the capacity of the grace of God in his life. He was able to put his past out of his mind and to press forward to his future.

I read bible stories differently nowadays. I know that behind every story are a lot of experiences, feelings and faith.

On the Potter's Wheel is where God picked up the pieces of my life and began to shape me into His work of art. It was His loving care that helped me to understand and fully appreciate how intimately He wants us to know Him. He loves us so much that He is not willing that we be lost.

The Conclusion

There will always be poor managers, situations and circumstances designed to get us off track. But, it is how we deal with these people or circumstances that will determine how God will deal with us. If we follow the Word of God and correct ourselves, God will not have to correct us. But, when there are areas in our life that is contrary to the Word of God or His will for us, God will bring correction when we ask Him to.

I am so thankful to God, I no longer see the loss instead, I remember the good times, the friends and the rewards of having had a wonderful career. More than anything else, I am thankful to God for His grace and mercy for allowing me to go further than I ever dreamed of again. With God, the good always outweighs the bad.

My future is bright! God is still molding me and shaping me. He is still teaching and training me. But today, I'm a willing vessel on the Potter's wheel.

ABOUT THE AUTHOR

Dr. Teresita Glasgow is an author, speaker, and coach; she is the president and CEO of In His Season, Inc., and the founder of Destiny Dreamer Coaching. Teresita has a wide range of professional experience which includes both the private and public sectors. She is best known for spending seventeen years navigating through the ranks of the male dominated financial services industry within Corporate Trust where she successfully went from a single parent on welfare to a Wall Street career. Beginning at the very bottom, she eventually became a Vice president, Relationship Manager and Certified Corporate Trust Specialist. Working in a fiduciary capacity, she has closed and managed multiple millions in bond financing deals and assets.

Drawing from her background in corporate and ministerial leadership, personal development, professional coaching and having a dynamic mindset, Dr. Glasgow uses communication and faith to transform the lives of others taking people from where they are to where they want to be.

Dr. Glasgow holds an Honorary Doctor of Divinity Degree from Trinity International University of Ambassadors and is a recipient of The Presidential Lifetime Achievement Award under President Barack Obama.

Connect with me on Social Media!

https://www.facebook.com/teresitaglasgow.page
http://www.teresitaglasgow.com/
http://destinydreamercoaching.com
http://www.inhisseason.com/

Dr. Teresita Glasgow

I Coach professional women to soar past their fears, free up their time, rediscover their dreams, and reignite their passion so they can live the life they've always dreamed of.

Destiny Dreamer Coaching
http://bit.ly/destinydc

Made in the USA
Columbia, SC
13 May 2019